Story Maps:
How to Write a GREAT Screenplay
by Daniel P. Calvisi

ACT FOUR SCREENPLAYS

To all of the aspiring screenwriters out there

who dream of turning their night job

into their day job.

ABOUT THE AUTHOR

Daniel P. Calvisi is a professional Story Analyst and screenwriter with over 15 years of experience focusing full-time on the craft and business of screenplays.

His employers have included Miramax Films, Dimension Films, Oscar-winning director Jonathan Demme and Twentieth Century Fox—he has evaluated written submissions for the executives who developed the films *Chicago, Spy Kids, Chocolat, Limitless, Scream, The Wedding Singer, The Game, One Fine Day* and *Ulee's Gold*.

Daniel has written screenplays on assignment and coached hundreds of private writers to better understand the principles of great screenwriting and to improve their craft on the written page. He has taught screenwriting and story analysis at the college level, including at the New School University in New York City.

Daniel has been published in *Script* magazine and is a contributor to *Now Write! Screenwriting*. He is the President of The Writers Building, an exclusive networking group and online community for professional screenwriters. Daniel lives in Los Angeles and he offers free downloads, classes, publications and consulting services at **ActFourScreenplays.com**.

INTRODUCTION

This book is the culmination of many years of working with screenplays and screenwriters. Reading, analyzing, evaluating, studying, teaching and coaching.

And, of course, writing. But it may interest you to know that although I get paid to write screenplays, I feel that the actual writing is the second most important educational tool for learning the craft. The first is <u>written</u> <u>analysis</u> of screenplays and movies, the good ones and the bad ones.

I learned this on the job working in the movie industry for years as a Story Analyst for many top studios and production companies and from working one-on-one with screenwriters, both amateur and professional.

Over a period of years, I developed the Story Map method of structural analysis, which can be used to construct a new narrative or deconstruct an existing one. I discovered the importance of not just hitting page points, but using what I call *Active Storytelling*, which is making your scenes and your characters' actions advance the story and bring about change while maintaining a cohesion built on theme and escalating conflict.

The purpose of the book is simple: to help you improve your craft and increase your odds of getting your script to impress a decision-maker in Hollywood. That's it.

This method is not a guarantee of success, or a way to sidestep the hard work of building your craft and developing your voice. It's a comprehensive working process that has guided hundreds of writers to craft their best work, and I'm excited and proud to bring it to you.

There are many books on screenwriting. So why this one?

- It's from the perspective of the person on the other side of the desk who evaluates your material. No matter where you're at in your career or who you know, you still need to blow away the reader, so I'm going to show you the best and most focused way to emulate the many successful scripts and movies that I've studied for over two decades.

- My structure system applies to every genre and the beats are *always in the same order*. There is no mixing and matching, order changes, or needless categorizing as with other systems. My method is stripped down to the practical essentials—let's leave the theory and the journal entries and the pats on the back behind—I'm preparing you for the market to get past brutal readers like myself.

- All of the analysis and guidelines in this book are based on the current, model spec screenplay in Hollywood. Lean, mean and fast-paced, this is not your uncle's screenplay – this is not a winking holdover from the "Boom-Boom" '80s and '90s (you know, when they were handing out spec deals at LAX?). This 100-110 page cinematic emotion machine has a very clear and clean set of guidelines, qualities and standards, some of which can be broken, but only if you've mastered them first.

- All of the advice (and the quotations, which you'll find in the "From The Trenches" sidebars) comes from my direct experience with working professionals in the movie industry. If I quote a source (other than the great Billy Wilder, R.I.P.), then it's because I personally spoke with them or was in the room when they spoke. These are exclusive bits of wisdom I've gathered from living and working in Los Angeles and New York City.

I'm going to strip it down.

I'm going to be tough on you.

I'm going to ask, "Are you a *real* writer?"

I'm going to show you many examples from produced screenplays written by top professionals. I'm going to keep up the pace and get to the point, with all the fat trimmed and focused only on the *crucial* information.

Just as I like my scripts.

Good Luck and Happy Writing!

Dan Calvisi

CONTENTS

I. VINCE VAUGHN IS DOING A SONG WITH THE BAND!

I attended the New York premiere of a film starring Vince Vaughn. Immediately upon entering the noisy after-party, I was told the buzz: Vince Vaughn was going to sing a song with the band!

Who's the band? Nobody knew. What song will he sing? Nobody knew. Does he know the band? Nothing. Has he ever sang or been in a band? Nada.

It didn't matter. This was why everyone, including me, was sticking around this boring party with no food and a cash bar.

I did a lap, saw a few celebs, and I was ready to go home. But nay! I had to see Vince Vaughn do a number with the band.

TWO HOURS LATER (on a weeknight, mind you) the band introduces Mr. Vaughn and he bounds onstage, picks up a mic and gives a bro-hug to the lead singer. So they start the song that no one recognizes...Vince Vaughn's lyrics are unintelligible...he doesn't do anything funny and looks a bit stiff, to be honest...and then the song ends and he disappears backstage.

The lights come up and everyone looks around with an expression like "That's it?"

The hall cleared out and everyone went back to their lives, having lost two hours of sleep, and the next day it was all forgotten.

*The Moral of the story: a big-name star can get them to show up, but if you really want them to remember your movie, you need to give them **a great story**.*

You must deliver...

II.   THE GREAT SCREENPLAY

Let's be clear.

You are not writing a masterpiece.

You are not writing your personal journey through life.

You are not writing a Best Picture winner.

You are writing a GREAT script in a commercially proven genre that will impress professional readers at the studio level in the film industry and establish your career.

Let's break that down.

Firstly, your screenplay can't just be good, or promising, or interesting. It must be GREAT.

It's not enough to have a really clever idea. Everyone in town has one of those (and some of them are downright brilliant). And when any of these idea-makers tells their idea to their friends, their friends say *Wow, that's a really clever idea!*

And it may, in fact, be a clever idea; even a *great* idea.

But it's not a great *script*. At least, not yet.

It's just a great concept.

And that's not enough to sell.

Thousands of pieces of writing are registered each year with the WGA registry and hundreds of scripts pour into Hollywood every week.

Hundreds every week. That's not even counting contests and internet services.

Your average studio Reader is given five scripts at a time. They get paid the same flat rate for each script. They stay up late, reading until all hours of the night to finish up those five scripts in two days (in between their other job/s, because you can't make a living as a Reader).

Most of what they read, about 90%, is crap. Maybe more.

What they are really looking for is that one great script that stands out from the dreck in the slush pile. The one to hook them and get them interested at 3:00 a.m.

That script with the GREAT opening page and the GREAT first ten pages and the GREAT turn on page 27 that they didn't see coming. And so on until that GREAT climactic confrontation.

And to top it all off...it's in the genre and budget range that their boss is looking for.

This is the beginning of a series of steps that can lead to meetings and more meetings and more submissions and rewrites and if the gods are smiling one day: a paycheck for the screenwriter.

Could happen. But it won't happen if you don't have the goods on the page. Unless your uncle is a studio head. Oh, wait, these days you want your uncle to be the CEO of a toy company, right? Yeah, that would be sweet. But if it's not the case, here's what you're going to do...

You're going to write a great script that will blow away that first reader, be they an official "Story Analyst" who will write up a coverage report...or an assistant...or a Creative Executive...or independent producer...or that assistant cameraman you met at the coffee shop who worked on a film with Phillip Seymour Hoffman and got to be really chummy with the Second A.D. who's *definitely* Phil's buddy and would *totally* slip him a script if he thought it was great. But the assistant cameraman has to read it first. Then the Second A.D. has to read it. Then Phil's manager's assistant's intern.

Then Phil's manager's assistant. Then Phil's manager. And then...the Oscar-winner himself will totally read your script. If it makes it that far up the ladder.

So how do you increase your odds to impress that many people with your screenplay?

To start, you're going to write in a commercially proven genre. I suggest writing in one of the staples — Thriller, Horror, Comedy, Action, Romantic Comedy, Drama. Right now, comedies seem to be the most consistent sellers, but comedy, as they say, is harder than dying. You don't have to be a funny person to write a successful comedy, you need something much more difficult: you need to be funny *on the page*.

A few years ago Horror was all the rage and now, at least at the studio level, it's barren. Who knows what will be selling like hotcakes tomorrow? No one does. So stick to a genre that you know and love. And don't chase whatever's hot at the box-office, because the industry is already one step beyond that.

A taut Thriller will *always* be marketable. A clever and funny RomCom can *never* go wrong. Stick to the staples and focus on writing a great script in your chosen genre.

This applies even if you have a connection to a Hollywood player. Here's a short list of people that clients of mine have had connections to (most through family members) and were planning to show their screenplays:

- James Cameron
- Francis Ford Coppola
- Ashton Kutcher
- Jennifer Lopez
- Rod Steiger

I told each of these writers that their scripts needed much more work. To date, I haven't read about any of them selling their scripts, even though I have no reason to doubt that they got their work into the offices of these power players. The reason is that their scripts were not ready. No one, not even your brother-in-law who is Jon Hamm's attorney, will risk their own reputation and career to pass on or purchase sub-par material.

You may be the ultimate guru of self-promotion and schmoozing, but once you shake hands with the big boys, you still need to deliver a great screenplay that will inspire them to spend years and millions to make into a great film.

Believe it or not, Hollywood readers do NOT want the same ol' thing. The CEOS and the marketing department may, but the development department does not. Or, if the company's development department has been gutted (you know, "the economy") then the few remaining Creative Executives crammed into that dusty cubicle still want something NEW and FRESH with an undeniable HOOK. And they are the ones who make careers. They want great *writers*.

I once asked a Junior Creative Executive, who is now the President of Production of Columbia Pictures, what she was looking for in a script and her answer was simple: "character." She wanted to find writers who wrote great characters so she could hire them to add strong characters to their screenplays that were already in development.

Even if they don't buy your spec, they may hire you to write one of their open assignments or they may get you some meetings, or an agent. This may, down the line, if you hang in there, lead to a paycheck. Could happen.

But I'll be honest, the odds are stacked against you. There are *so* many factors that go into a script sale, like...

- Who you know

- Your representation

- Talent attachments

- Financing

- Your personality and determination

- Getting it to the right people

- Timing of your concept and subject matter

Some of these are completely out of your control.

So what can you do to increase your odds in the marketplace? You can work on the one thing you have control over.

The quality of your work.

There's still no guarantee that your script will sell. In fact, I've read several screenplays that *did* sell...and I can safely say that many of my friends and clients have written much stronger scripts. Obviously, there were other factors helping these screenplays that meant more than the quality of the material at the time of submission.

So...good screenplays don't always sell.

Some bad screenplays sell.

It's a very tough business to break into with a ton of competition.

So why bother? Why put yourself through it?

Because if you're like me, you *have* to write.

You have those voices in your head.

You've probably tried to walk away from this crazy pursuit at some point in the past, maybe more than once; but you just can't do it. Like Michael Corleone, every time you try to get away from your screenplay, it pulls you back in!

You know the odds, but you're going to do it anyway because those voices won't leave you alone. Right? I hope so, because it's way too much work to approach lightly and it's foolhardy to think you can make a quick, easy buck at this pursuit.

So let's try to make it as good as it can be, in the style, form and format of the best movies coming out today, with the exact structure and pacing on the page that I know for certain all industry readers look for.

Know that the rules are different for *you* than they are for the big guys and gals at the top. You have to work harder for a smaller chunk of a smaller pie until you reach their lofty heights. Forget about collecting the big payday to write the *re-boot* of the *remake* of the Saturday morning cartoon based on the toy line from the early 1960s that was inspired by the hit movie from the mid-1950s that was really just a retelling of the classic folktale that desperately needs updating for the Youtube generation. They only give those jobs to the same batch of high-profile writers in town.

In other words, they already have a bunch of scribes they pay handsomely to write the same ol' schlock. You have to do better.

You have to give them what they didn't know they needed.

If you're serious about your craft, and you're in this for the long haul, you'll focus on writing the best script you can, to start impressing industry folks so you can get those meetings and snag that rep and scrape and claw your way toward actually making some money at this nutso endeavor.

But it has to get past that first reader if it's going anywhere.

I know, because I was a Senior Story Analyst who was given material from the top agents and producers with top actors attached. And it wasn't my job to show deference to an established pro – I evaluated each script on its own, as an anonymous piece of writing that aspired to be a movie for my employer. I was very tough; in fact, I was once referred to by a producer as "That reader that hates everything." (Which wasn't true. By "everything" he unwittingly meant the multiple scripts submitted by *his* company).

I've read screenplays at every level of competence and I've evaluated them for major movie companies and I've spent many years working with writers like you to help shape your material to make it blow away picky bastards like me.

And I'm telling you: it can't just be "good." It has to be <u>great</u>. Because all that matters is if that Reader wants to turn the page at 3:00 a.m. That's it.

Your goal is not to write a script like every other script in Hollywood or like the current reigning box-office champ. Your goal is to increase your chances of launching a screenwriting career by following certain established norms, procedures and techniques that are used every day by working writers in the industry and to write your butt off until you've mastered these techniques and produced something that won't just drop through the transom but kick the friggin' door down. That's it.

You can spend years writing and producing an avant-garde short film that will dazzle film festival audiences if that makes you happy. If you enjoy being creative in a particular way, whatever your chosen medium, then you should do that because it keeps you happy and it lowers stress levels. But if you're interested in working as a creative professional in the movie and television industry, I suggest you study and practice these techniques. So what's in a truly great screenplay? Here's a list of the major attributes...

THE GREAT SCREENPLAY (in no particular order of awesomeness):

- Fantastic CONCEPT

- COMMERCIAL appeal to a specific AUDIENCE

- Strong STORY ENGINES

- Fascinating and likeable PROTAGONIST

- Unique GOALS

- ACTIVE DECISIONS made by protagonist

- Escalating CONFLICT and STAKES

- Focused CONTROLLING THEME expressed in action

- Strong Classical four-act STRUCTURE

- Fast PACING

- Medium LENGTH (100 – 110 pages)

- Great OPENING

- Strong MIDPOINT

- Urgent time deadline: a "CLOCK"

- Great, satisfying, inevitable CLIMAX

- Passionate EXECUTION with an effective VOICE

- LOW to mid-range BUDGET

- SPECTACLE

Easy, huh? Just do all of that and boom: a Classic for the ages. You've got Ridley holding on line three.

Yes, your script is so bad-ass you've got Ridley ON HOLD.

Okay, you got me: it's not *quite* that easy.

In fact, each one of those categories in the Great Screenplay list represents a great deal of study and practice. To truly understand each element starts with the knowledge and method outlined in this book.

It's going to be tough. It's going to be rough. But it's also going to be *exhilarating*.

Ready? Good.

I mean...Great!

THE CONCEPT

III.   THE BIG IDEA

Your clever idea is not the only thing that will get you an option or sale—you still need top-quality execution—but it may be what gets your script in the door.

It's okay to write that memoir about your summer with Gram and Gramps to get it out of your system and learn the craft, but if you're looking to produce a more commercial spec script, you want to come up with a great idea that really hooks someone to think, "Now that's a movie I'd pay to see." Or even just, "I need to read this to see how the writer pulls it off."

I once attended a seminar in which a speaker said that you should only write a script that you feel would appeal to at least one million people. It was a good point – if your concept would only appeal to a tiny fringe of an audience, then it's probably not a commercial script for the spec market. Maybe skip it and move on to a concept with more broad appeal, or write it to produce as a self-financed indie film?

I hear the term "The Big Idea" used more often these days than the classic term "High Concept," but they essentially mean the same thing: a story concept that is easily understood in a few words and is undeniable in its compelling cleverness.

FROM THE TRENCHES:

GRAHAM YOST (*Speed, Broken Arrow, Band of Brothers, Justified*)

"You've got to be smart. You can't deliver on size and scope, so you need to deliver on intensity. And that's what a film like *Taken* does."

The Big Idea is...

- The first and perhaps the only thing that will get your script read if you're a new and unproven writer.

- A unique take on a commercially proven genre that no one's thought of yet.

- A new take on a universal theme or idea that would appeal to a broad audience around the world.

- <u>Not</u> just a stringing-together of familiar elements from other hit movies.

With so many franchise films and movies based on previously established material being made, it's tougher now than ever for you to sell your original spec screenplay. But one thing that hasn't changed: the need for a *Big Idea*!

From Jeffrey Katzenberg's famous memo from 1991:

"In the dizzying world of moviemaking, we must not be distracted from one fundamental concept: *the idea is king*...If a movie begins with a great, original idea, chances are good it will be successful, even if it is executed only marginally well. However if a film begins with a flawed idea, it will almost certainly fail, even if it is made with "A" talent and marketed to the hilt."

Coming from the studio head who green-lit *Pretty Woman*, *The Lion King* and *Shrek*, I'll take that advice.

Katzenberg goes on to talk about the term High Concept...

"'High Concept' is a useful, complex, thoughtful encapsulation of what we should all be working toward... It embellishes the concept that "the idea is king" by asserting that the idea that forms the basis of a film should not only be one that is compelling but also one that can be communicated.

The real meaning of high concept is that ingenuity is more important than production values. This is why we should constantly be looking for creative solutions, not financial ones."

I also like the way it's defined by Jerrol LeBaron, founder of Inktip.com:

"A high concept script should have a great title, a strong hook, and shouldn't have an overly complex plot. In addition to these elements, if your story cannot be described in one short simple sentence, it is not high concept."

HOOK ME

High Concept...The Big Idea...whatever you call it, it's gotta have a HOOK. A twist on a familiar or classic character/scenario.

Here are three relatively recent films that were sold as specs or pitches. Each one sports a very clear and dynamic hook:

Armored – When five armored guards rob their own shipment of $8 million and an innocent man is killed, the rookie in the bunch locks himself in the armored vehicle...with the money.

The Hangover – A group of guys wake up in Vegas the morning after their bachelor party with no memory of the night before and the groom is missing.

No Strings Attached (Note: the script was originally named *F**kbuddies,* a title that everyone in town knew was not releasable but made sure that everyone in town wanted to read it!) – A guy and a girl make a pact to use each other for meaningless sex...until true feelings arise.

Take a look at John Hughes films for a bunch of fantastic Big Ideas:

- Five teens, all strangers and from different circles, spend a Saturday in detention and bond as they battle their tyrannical school principal.

- A popular teenage kid and his two friends have the ultimate ditch day from school as they are stalked by the principal.

- Two teenage virgins create a sexy woman with their computer.

- A recently laid-off father must become a stay-at-home dad while his wife joins the work force.

- Two strangers get stranded during a blizzard and must travel cross-country together by car to get home for Christmas.

- A young boy gets left behind by his family and must defend his house from two burglars.

Here are some Big Ideas that we all wish we could have invented:

Shakespeare in Love – A comedic "re-writing of history" in which a young William Shakespeare is inspired by his own tortured romance to write "Romeo and Juliet," the most famous fictional romance in history.

Slumdog Millionaire – A kid who grew up in extreme poverty uses his memories to answer the questions on the quiz show, "Who Wants to Be A Millionaire?"

Minority Report – The police officer who oversees the department that predicts future murders must go on the run when the system predicts he is the next killer.

Ransom – A father decides to offer the $1 million ransom as a bounty on the head of his son's kidnappers.

The Others – A family plagued by a haunted house turn out to be the ghosts haunting the real family that lives in the house.

Extract – A guy stuck in a sexless marriage hires a young gigolo to seduce his wife so he can justify his own affair, guilt-free.

Here are four high-concept scripts that sold in recent years...

Swingles – A "wingwoman" helps a guy pick up girls in bars.

Buried – A man is buried in a coffin with only his cell phone.

The Days Before – A man from the future keeps hopping one successive day into the past, desperate to stop a vicious race of time-traveling aliens from wiping out humanity.

Allies With Benefits – The female President of The United States falls for her old college fling, the new Prime Minister of England.

PRE-EXISTING ELEMENTS AND ARCHETYPES

Here are some more, but see if you can spot a pattern this time...

Nottingham – A re-imagining of the Robin Hood story told from the perspective of the Sheriff.

Goliath – A re-imagining of the David and Goliath story as an action movie that creates an expanded origin of the giant Goliath.

The Curse Of Medusa – A re-imagining of the myth that creates an expanded origin story for Medusa the Gorgon.

Snow White And The Huntsman – A re-imagining of the story of Snow White in which the huntsman sent to kill her becomes her mentor.

Hyde – A re-imagining of the classic story in which an allegedly rehabilitated Dr. Jekyll is pulled out of prison to help hunt a new monster who seems to be using an improved version of the Hyde serum.

Hollywood sure loves its re-imaginings, huh? They're always looking for the new take on a classic story, especially when it's in the public domain like myths and fairy tales. That means they don't have to pay for the rights.

The lesson here is that it's wise to build your concept from a universal story — a myth, fairy tale, historical event, public figure or pop culture archetype that is known by millions.

Here are three dynamic big ideas that hinge on very recognizable elements. I'm not saying they're *great* ideas—to each his own—just that the hooks have a very high recognition factor:

Abraham Lincoln: Vampire Hunter – When the mother of future United States President Abraham Lincoln is murdered by a vampire, he begins a lifelong vendetta to rid the world of the heinous creatures.

Roundtable – Four modern-day knights (i.e., celebrities, not warriors) find themselves called upon to save the planet from an ancient evil force.

Comic Con – To save their beloved neighborhood comic shop, a Justice League of geeks must plan and execute a daring heist at Comic-Con.

Execution-Dependent

There are some big ideas that are so quirky and unique, they are said to be "execution-dependent." In other words, it's a great idea *if* it's a great script, but a horrible idea if it's not.

For example:

The Beaver – a man wakes up with a beaver puppet fused onto his hand and he begins to speak through it with a British accent.

The screenplay for *The Beaver* is quite well-executed, but considering the concept is very difficult to communicate outside of the screenplay, it could have been a disaster and not sold.

Charlie Kaufman (*Being John Malkovich, Eternal Sunshine of the Spotless Mind, Synecdoche, New York*) is an example of a writer who can deliver something wholly original and downright odd and have it be considered commercial because he's a marquee name. For a new writer, however, you don't have a track record to lean on and you just want to get someone to read your script; this will be much easier if there are some recognizable elements in your logline.

THE STRUCTURE

Definition of Story Maps

A Story Map is a method for structuring a screenplay by creating a simple yet powerful outline that contains the building blocks of your concept, characters and plot: the main dramatic elements and dramatic beats of the narrative and the order and desired page range of those beats, regardless of genre.

95% of great movies follow the Story Map.

Honestly, if we're talking about commercial, wide-release Hollywood movies, I might bump that up to 100%. It's rare to find one that doesn't use a four act structure with the elements and plot beats described below.

With that said, I'd like to issue a formal challenge: find a commercial, narrative feature film to come from a major studio in the past 10 years that does *not* follow the Story Map. Email me your map for the film and I'll analyze it; if you're right, I'll print your name and analysis on my blog (which, as many of you already know, is the equivalent of a Knighthood in the UK). You may then bask in the glory of having proved me wrong. *If* you can, that is. With that gauntlet thrown, let's continue.

In the beat sheet of a Story Map, I define each plot point down to <u>the page</u>. Because that's how the pros do it and that's exactly what I was looking for as a reader working for major studios and production companies. Believe it or not, it actually mattered to me if a script's Inciting Incident (to be defined soon) fell on page 8-10 rather than 12-13. It made a big difference in the pacing of the first act, and it showed me whether this was a writer with the discipline to cut down on "setup" and suck me in, or this was a writer who failed to recognize the urgency of a movie narrative and the intense competition of the script marketplace. Which writer would you rather be?

Form, Not Formula

The Story Map is <u>not</u> a formula. It is a story structure that is followed by almost every popular Hollywood film. It does not dictate your choices; it only provides a framework to hold your choices.

This is not a machine for making "cookie-cutter" movies; unless you consider *Transformers, Sideways, The Hangover* and *Frozen River* to be cut from the same mold, because they all utilize the Full Story Map.

Even so, I know there will be doubters out there.

I've seen the message boards where an angry, frustrated writer inevitably blames the lack of imagination in Hollywood on structure paradigms in screenwriting books. I whole-heartedly agree that the major studios and many of the independents are putting way too much emphasis on the so-called "franchise films" and pre-existing source material and not investing enough in original stories, but this has nothing to do with a dearth of good writing or the reliance on classic structural forms. It has to do with economics and a lack of creative vision at the management level of corporate movie companies.

When using the Story Map, the screenplay is still undeniably yours, but it now comes wrapped in the shiny coating that covers pretty much all major studio movies and is recognized by every agent, manager and producer in the business.

In fact, I think that it shows *more* skill to write a great script within the confines of a classically structured, 110 page format. You're not re-inventing the wheel, you're building the best wheel that we've yet seen. Think of it like architecture – building designs are limitless, but they all contain walls, a roof, an entrance and windows. Crafting a building that uses those necessary features doesn't limit your design, at all. It's precisely *how* the gifted architects throughout history have used those elements in a new, undeniably creative manner that has distinguished geniuses like Frank Lloyd Wright, I.M. Pei and Frank Gehry.

But right now, I guarantee you that there are several film students around the globe attempting to create a hybrid screenplay structure that combines standard script format with the novel and poetry. They're doing this before they even understand the fundamentals of any of these forms, and they're wasting their time.

Simply put, if you follow the Story Map and execute an active story in the proper page ranges, your script will *feel* like a modern hit movie.

IV.   THE "BASIC" STORY MAP

After years of professional story analysis, the Story Map is
the only method of narrative construction and
deconstruction that I use, and I believe it can find what is
working or *not* working in any form (screenplay, teleplay,
novel, short story, etc.).

Have you ever had that experience where you watch a film or
read a story and something is "wrong," but you can't put
your finger on it? On the surface, it seems to be well-
crafted, but for whatever reason, you know the story took a
wrong turn or made a decision that didn't feel organic.

The story is probably missing one of the Basic Story Map
elements, or the elements do not generate conflict so the
drama is not there. After all, DRAMA = CONFLICT, so we want
our Story Map to create a combustible mix.

The Basic Story Map compiles your main dramatic elements.
In short, the Basic Story Map outlines:

- The protagonist

- The protagonist's goals

- What keeps the protagonist from reaching the goals

- What the story is about

- How the protagonist changes

- How the story ends

- How the story is captured in a single, dynamic
  sentence

Your entire narrative flows from these building blocks of
your story. Your main throughline (or story "spine") usually
flows from your protagonist's pursuit of his/her External

Goal. The opening and ending of your story and the arc of your protagonist are often dictated by your Theme. The protagonist's dialogue is often influenced by their skill and misbehavior. The fascinating mystery that the audience hopes will be solved is defined by the Central Dramatic Question. The list goes on.

The Basic Story Map elements are vital and absolutely crucial to *any* story. Often, a screenplay or film does not work because one or more of these vital elements is missing.

How many times have we seen a brainless action or horror movie that just wasn't *about* anything? There was not a clear Theme to add cohesion to the various set pieces or resonance to the CGI sequences. How about a movie where the protagonist isn't likeable? This could be because they have no Internal Goal to show the emotional side of their character...or maybe their External Goal is inherently immoral...or the antagonist is not directly in conflict with the protagonist. Ever been sitting in the theater, just waiting for the movie to <u>end</u>? It's racing to the big climax and you just...don't...care. This may be because they already answered the Central Dramatic Question so there's no mystery left to be solved.

To create your Basic Story Map, you must define these elements:

1) **PROTAGONIST**: The main character; age, occupation, status

> **Skill**: What they're good at

> **Misbehavior**: A trait or quirk that consistently generates conflict

> **Flaw/Achilles Heel**: Their weakness that causes them to fail until they are able to overcome it

2) EXTERNAL GOAL: The plot goal/action goal

3) INTERNAL GOAL: The character goal/emotional goal

4) MAIN DRAMATIC CONFLICT: What's keeping them from the goal/ the Antagonist (villain)/ the major problem

5) CONTROLLING THEME: What is this story about? What are you saying? What idea is being explored and revealed?

6) CENTRAL DRAMATIC QUESTION: The main question the story seeks to answer/the mystery

7) ENDING: How the story comes to a climax and the resolution that follows

8) ARC: The change your protagonist goes through (or powerful realization they come to) from start to finish of the story

Ideally, these elements all GENERATE CONFLICT. No one wants to watch a romance wherein two lovers from the same social class meet, fall in love, court one another with no complications and get married. We want *Romeo & Juliet*, where the two lovers come from warring families. Or *Titanic*, where Rose is wealthy and betrothed to a horrible man in her own social class but she falls in love with Jack, a scrappy vagabond with only 5 bucks in his pocket. (Oh, and the ship is sinking so their decisions literally become a question of life and death.)

So think about Conflict when you construct your main elements, and think about what you want to say (your Theme) because you want these elements to support that theme. *Slumdog Millionaire* is about destiny and fate, so the story focuses on a near-impossible task: JAMAL, an uneducated boy from the slums has a chance to win a million dollars on a quiz show *and* win over a girl betrothed to a murderous gangster. See how he's pulled between the two worlds of his past and his future, poverty and riches? These two pursuits are his External and Internal Goals.

What's standing in Jamal's way? What's *not* standing in his way? Is it his destiny to win both the money and the girl? Well, this is Hollywood, so, um, yeah.

Bruce Wayne is faced with an impossible choice in *The Dark Knight*. To stop the Joker from destroying Gotham City, he must either kill him, which he has sworn not to do, or reveal his true identity as the Batman, which would destroy Batman and return Gotham City to criminal infestation.

In *How to Lose a Guy in 10 Days*, a magazine columnist must get a guy to dump her in 10 days to meet a deadline...and the guy must get her to fall in love with him in 10 days to win a lucrative ad account. Clear, opposing goals that generate high conflict.

In *Alice In Wonderland (2010)*, Alice's skill is that she has a wonderful imagination. All of the villains in the piece are trying to harness her imagination and subjugate her. Her father, the only person who encouraged her imagination, dies and Alice becomes a lone underdog in search of her true self. Is she *the* Alice from the prophecy? She needs to decide at some point in order to realize her destiny. In short, she needs to take control and grow up as this is a coming-of-age tale – this is reflected in the real world as she flees the engagement ceremony that was thrust upon her and then in the fantasy world as she is thrust into the role of savior to fight the terrible dragon. As in other "prophecy/The One" stories such as *The Matrix*, *Unforgiven* and *Star Wars Episode One: The Phantom Menace*, her arc is to "become the myth" that has been foretold about her. The seeds of this transformation must be in the Basic Story Map.

Here's a sample from another story of a girl who needs to grow up...

JUNO

Screenplay written by Diablo Cody

101 pages

BASIC STORY MAP

PROTAGONIST: JUNO MACGUFF, pregnant teen girl

    Skill: Sarcastic

    Misbehavior: Smart mouth, bleak outlook

    Flaw: Naive

EXTERNAL GOAL: To have the baby and give it to the Lorings.

INTERNAL GOAL: To get together with Paulie.

MAIN DRAMATIC CONFLICT: Bren (her step-mother) and Mark Loring

THEME: Finding and appreciating true love

CENTRAL DRAMATIC QUESTION: Can Juno find a happy home for her baby and get together with Paulie?

THE ENDING: Juno gives the baby to Vanessa Loring and gets together with Paulie.

ARC: Juno goes from a frightened loner to finding true love with Paulie.

LOGLINE: A pregnant teen must decide between giving her baby to an unstable yuppie couple or keeping it with her estranged high school boyfriend.

I highly suggest you write down your Basic Story Map and have it taped up beside your computer (or in an open file on your computer) for quick reference. It may seem like many of the above elements in *Juno* are simple and obvious, something Diablo Cody could have easily kept in mind as she wrote it, but that's an assumption made *after* you've seen the film. For the writer writing a script for the first time, or even in subsequent drafts, it can only help to have a constant reminder of the controlling elements to execute the best interpretation of the initial concept.

For example, if you're in doubt as to the actions or dialogue of your protagonist in a given scene, then go back to your Theme and their External Goal. Are they expressing the theme by taking actions to pursue their goal or is this scene just filler?

Bottom line, you must define your Basic Story Map to write a FOCUSED story. The goal is a COHESIVE story, wherein each element is organic, generates conflict and advances the story. We'll look at more examples of the Basic Story Map in a bit.

THE LOGLINE

The logline is the final element in the Basic Story Map. You may create your logline before the other Basic Story Map elements or after. Either way, it's incredibly important.

Your logline, essentially your story in approximately 25 words or less, showcases your unique dramatic situation, your main character and the compelling conflict that keeps them from their goal.

Drafting a strong logline before you write your screenplay will help you to "find" your story, especially your throughline (main line of action, usually the protagonist's pursuit of their External Goal) and your HOOK (the unique twist on the genre or classic archetype that will compel someone to read the script).

A logline is also used in the industry for marketing purposes – to "pitch" your completed spec script in the hopes of gaining a submission request. Instead of figuring out the best logline after you're done with the script, you're going to BEGIN with crafting a kick-butt logline that sounds like a GREAT STORY and a BIG IDEA that would garner requests for submission.

By crafting your logline and showing it to friends and trusted industry professionals for feedback before you start writing script pages, you won't fall into the trap of spending months crafting a screenplay that's unfocused, uncommercial and unwieldy.

SEEDS OF THE STORY

First and foremost, the Logline communicates the main "story engine" of the film: what drives the narrative. Each act will have its own specific story engine, but your story needs a main *throughline* or *story spine* to hold it together and on track. For example...

A detective must find and capture a serial killer.

A lovelorn woman must find a date for her sister's wedding.

A child must escape a haunted house.

But that's not enough. A great logline is <u>specific</u>. A great logline captures a fascinating main character in only a few words.

The detective is a petite female trainee.

The lovelorn woman has written several books on...love.

The child is blind.

A great logline showcases a unique HOOK: the special element/s that make your take on this material unique. Think about what makes your concept...

- Relevant to our times

- A new take on a classic story or proven genre

- A unique and cohesive melding of familiar elements

- A funny situation

- An impossible yet compelling scenario

You may have heard the term "familiar but different." This can be an accurate depiction of some hit movies and a helpful term, but don't fall into the habit of just plucking elements from other movies in a bid to make your script more "commercial."

A *great idea* is commercial.

Great writing is commercial.

A *fresh hook* is commercial.

When I was working as a reader, I made a point not to approach a new script looking for a reason to say "No." I was looking for reasons to say "Yes!" I had to read so much dreck that I was dying to find something with a brilliant concept and great execution. That's why I like to say...

CRAFT = CAREER

The first and most important step to establishing a career is developing your screenwriting craft. In this age of pitchfests, script contests and "logline blast services" that convince a lot of new writers to start marketing their work before it's ready, the one thing you can truly control is your craft, the quality of your work.

And as you practice your execution on the page, your ideas will also improve since you will be developing your ability to choose the most dynamic concept out of a batch of ideas.

After all, you don't know if those contacts you made at that film festival will actually help your career. You never know how long it will take an agent or executive to read your script or if they'll even bother to return a response. You can't predict how anyone will react to your material. All of this is completely out of your control.

All you can do is write the best script you can write. And it all begins with your logline, which you want to leap out at the Reader so they say "Now *that* would make a great movie" or "Why didn't I think of that?" Something like...

An obsessive-compulsive, homophobic novelist must help his gay artist neighbor in order to win over the single mother he secretly loves. [22 words]

A failed child psychologist must help a young boy who is haunted by ghosts. [14 words]

A washed-up boxer from South Philly gets a shot at a title fight against the heavyweight champion of the world. [21 words]

A female FBI trainee must enlist the aid of a brilliant, imprisoned serial killer to catch another serial killer-at-large. [21 words]

I list the number of words in those sentences so you can see how many dramatic elements you can fit into such a short line.

Some of you may think you need more words to capture your story, or you don't understand the true focus and purpose of the logline so you write a 3-line, 55-word logline. I'm sorry to break it to thee, kindly screenwriter, but nay, your script is *not* the rare script that DEMANDS that many words! Stick to 20-30 words and you'll soon find out if your concept is clear and concise.

And you'll notice that I don't give away the endings in these loglines. I prefer a logline that hooks me in with the promise of an interesting hero, a dramatic situation injected with high stakes and a mystery that I want to see solved. In short, *it makes me want to read the script*.

WHAT'S THE STORY?

The Logline's goal is <u>to get someone to read the script</u>. That's it.

The Logline focuses on <u>the story</u>, not on genre, marketing or box-office.

A logline is NOT a tagline. A tagline is advertising copy used to sell a movie, for example...

No one in space can hear you scream.

Truth has a soldier.

This summer, stuff blows up.

You don't want to tell them how to sell your movie. You're the writer, you are *not* the marketing department. Toward this end, don't mention other movies in your logline; again, stick to your story.

For the record, I think it's okay to mention other films in a cover letter but I'd avoid them in a logline. It's fine to mention in a conversation or in an email that your script's tone is reminiscent of *Crash,* or it could be described as "The Sixth Sense meets The Dark Knight" if a) your description/movie mash-up makes sense (this example does not) and b) you have already communicated your compelling logline, which will show them the crucial details of the story.

If you're just starting your screenplay, I would suggest you craft a strong logline FIRST, make sure it pops, then build your story to reflect it. And if you're rewriting a completed draft, then I suggest you also craft a stronger logline and rewrite your story to fit this logline. This will force you to use an active structure.

LET'S DO IT

There is more than one template for a successful logline, but I use the following basic construction:

An engaging protagonist must struggle against tremendous odds to achieve his/her goal.

In that sentence you have many of the Basic Story Map elements: what makes the main character unique (*engaging protagonist*), what is <u>forcing</u> them to act and how they take action (*<u>must</u> struggle*), the main dramatic conflict they struggle against (*tremendous odds*), and what they want (*goal*).

Again, you can draft your logline after you write your Basic Story Map or shape your Basic Story Map to reflect your logline. It's up to you.

This construction emphasizes that your protagonist is taking action – they are pushing the story forward with their active struggle against escalating conflict. Your hero should be the subject of the sentence. You don't want to craft a logline in which the subject is an event, the villain or your theme. For example, here's some hypothetical <u>weak loglines</u> for movies with strong concepts...

An alien invasion takes Earth by surprise and they must fight back. (Independence Day?)

Darth Vader chases a band of adventurers led by Luke Skywalker who wants to protect secret plans for the Death Star from the evil Empire. (Star Wars?)

*A story about what happens when a loser gets a
successful, beautiful woman pregnant. (Knocked Up?)*

None of these loglines are specific, actively structured or tell
us what is unique about the protagonist. The first two have
pronoun-verb agreement problems so they are just plain
confusing.

It's important to structure your logline around an active
protagonist. Stories with passive protagonists, who do not
take action but rather react to external conflict, are very
difficult to tell successfully and often end up as unsatisfying
experiences for the reader and audience. They are a frequent
beginner mistake, most often contain numerous story
problems and they are not advised for the new writer.

THE GENRE

I suggest that you list the genre above your logline
so the other party is clear on what kind of movie
this is. In many cases, a concept can be interpreted
in different ways, so it helps to know the genre as
you read the logline.

It's always best to err on the side of clarity — don't assume
they know or understand anything about your story. It's not
always as clear as you may think (which is why it's so
important to get objective opinions on your logline as well
as your screenplay).

For example, if the title is *Cereal Killer*, we're pretty sure it's
a comedy. But if it's *Serial Killer*, it could go multiple ways:

SERIAL KILLER
Thriller
When a ruthless killer begins to murder people in a small
town, a paperboy realizes the victims are all on his route and
he's the only one who can stop him.

SERIAL KILLER
Comedy
When a ruthless killer begins to murder people in a small
town, a paperboy realizes the victims are all on his route and
he's the only one who can stop him!

It's not the best worded logline, but it's just an example of
how the same pitch can be construed in different ways. The
first one could be a thriller from the Coen brothers, and the
second one could be a satire from the Farrelly brothers.
(Either way, it's apparent that the film must be directed by
siblings!)

SAMPLE BASIC STORY MAPS

Here's a sample Basic Story Map for the dramatic comedy *As
Good as it Gets*, which uses the device of the "False Goal" as
this is a protagonist who doesn't know what's good for him;
Melvin Udall (Jack Nicholson) does not realize that he is in
fact on a righteous path toward improving his life. (As
opposed to, say, a revenge story like *Gladiator* (see below)
where Maximus embarks on a righteous quest, and his
intentions are never questioned.)

AS GOOD AS IT GETS

written by Mark Andrus and James L. Brooks

BASIC STORY MAP:

PROTAGONIST: MELVIN UDALL, 50s, shut-in wealthy novelist
in NYC

> **Skill:** His biting and terrible wit

> **Misbehavior:** racist/sexist/homophobic/obsessive-
> compulsive

> **Achilles Heel:** He has a soft heart deep down

FALSE GOAL: To isolate himself

EXTERNAL GOAL: To belittle Simon / To make friends with him

INTERNAL GOAL: To use Carol / To win over Carol as a girlfriend

(note: The slash in the External and Internal Goals represents the Midpoint, which in this case is the transition from False Goal to True Goal.)

MAIN DRAMATIC CONFLICT: Melvin's pessimism

THEME: Don't let pessimism rule you.

CENTRAL DRAMATIC QUESTION: Will Melvin accept his gay neighbor and get together with Carol? (In essence, can he achieve human intimacy?)

ENDING: Melvin offers Simon his home and takes his advice to pursue Carol -- he goes to Carol and they get together.

ARC: Melvin goes from isolationist jerk to friend and lover, learning that to receive happiness and support he must first give of himself.

LOGLINE: An obsessive-compulsive, homophobic novelist must help his gay artist neighbor in order to win over the single mother he secretly loves.

From the above, we can see the foundation of the general structure of the story: Melvin consciously pushes toward isolating himself through selfish actions, while unconsciously bringing him closer to others.

Here's a slightly more straightforward set of elements for the period action revenge picture *Gladiator*. Note how there are two major themes here, both of which come to fruition in the ending. Also, Maximus does not go through much internal change in the course of the story; thus, there is a huge external change: he dies and Rome is returned to a republic.

GLADIATOR

Screenplay by David Franzoni, John Logan
and William Nicholson

BASIC STORY MAP

PROTAGONIST: MAXIMUS, 40s, Roman general, loving father

Skill: Great warrior

Misbehavior: Disrespect for politicians

Achilles Heel: Impulsive

EXTERNAL GOAL: To get revenge on Commodus, the young Caesar

INTERNAL GOAL: To "go home"/achieve spiritual peace

THEMES: The afterlife (living with honor)/ Republic vs. Autocracy

MAIN DRAMATIC CONFLICT: Commodus

ENDING: Maximus kills Commodus in a gladiator battle before he dies from blood loss, ascending to heaven. Rome is restored to a republic.

CENTRAL DRAMATIC QUESTION: Will Maximus defeat Commodus and achieve peace in his soul?

ARC: Maximus goes from a celebrated Roman general to a slave to an honorable death, joining his family in heaven.

LOGLINE: When a Roman general's family is murdered and he is made a slave after a coup, he must survive brutal gladiator matches in order to get revenge on the young Emperor.

In the comedy *The Hangover*, there are three main characters, but my choice for the Protagonist would be the one who goes through the most change: Stu, played by Ed Helms.

THE HANGOVER
Written by Jon Lucas & Scott Moore

BASIC STORY MAP

PROTAGONIST: STU, dentist

> **Misbehavior:** Constantly worried and always sees the worst
>
> **Skill:** Nice guy
>
> **Flaw/Achilles Heel:** He's a wimp

EXTERNAL GOAL: To find Doug (the groom)

INTERNAL GOAL: To dump his awful girlfriend Melissa

MAIN DRAMATIC CONFLICT: Their memory loss and previous night's antics

THEME: Loyalty and True Friendship

CENTRAL DRAMATIC QUESTION: Can the guys find Doug in time for the wedding, and can Stu find love?

ENDING: Stu breaks up with Melissa at the wedding, and the guys look at photos from the weekend.

ARC: Stu goes from a wimpy victim to a take-charge guy with a promising romantic life.

LOGLINE: A group of friends with no memory of their sordid bachelor party must piece together the events of the night to find the missing groom before the wedding the next day.

V. MORE ON THE BASIC STORY MAP WITH EXAMPLES

Let's review the Basic Story Map elements in more detail with examples from five classic films; some are obvious, others, unconventional.

1) PROTAGONIST:

The main character; age, occupation, status

> **Skill**: What they're good at
>
>> *Indiana Jones* (Raiders of the Lost Ark)*: Adventurer and Archaeologist*
>>
>> *Will Hunting* (Good Will Hunting)*: Math genius*
>>
>> *Clarice Starling* (The Silence of the Lambs)*: Detective skills*
>>
>> *Frankie Dunn* (Million Dollar Baby)*: Boxing training*
>>
>> *Greg Focker* (Meet The Parents): *Kindness*
>
> **Misbehavior**: A trait or quirk that consistently generates conflict
>
>> *Indiana Jones: Impulsive*
>>
>> *Will Hunting: Bad temper*
>>
>> *Clarice Starling: Impulsive and Petite*
>>
>> *Frankie Dunn: Afraid to take a risk*
>>
>> *Greg Focker: Lying*
>
> **Flaw/Achilles Heel**: Their weakness that makes them fail until they are able to overcome it
>
>> *Indiana Jones: Afraid of snakes*
>>
>> *Will Hunting: Fear of leaving his old identity*
>>
>> *Clarice Starling: Ambition*
>>
>> *Frankie Dunn: Needs a daughter to love*

Greg Focker: Needs to please his father-in-law

2) EXTERNAL GOAL:

The plot goal/action goal, often generates the main throughline or "spine" of the story

Indiana Jones: To recover the ark.

Will Hunting: To complete his required therapy sessions.

Clarice Starling: To catch Buffalo Bill.

Frankie Dunn: To train a champion.

Greg Focker: To win over his father-in-law, Jack

3) INTERNAL GOAL:

The character goal/emotional goal; often the love interest, central relationship or personal problem that they must overcome

Indiana Jones: To support and protect Marion.

Will Hunting: To be honest with his girlfriend, Skylar.

Clarice Starling: To get out of her father's shadow.

Frankie Dunn: To support and protect Maggie.

Greg Focker: To propose to Pam.

4) MAIN DRAMATIC CONFLICT:

What's keeping them from the goal/ the Antagonist (villain)/ the major problem

Raiders of the Lost Ark: *Belloq/The Nazi's*

Good Will Hunting: *Sean, his therapist*

The Silence of the Lambs: *Hannibal Lecter*

Million Dollar Baby: *Maggie*

Meet The Parents: *Jack*

5) CONTROLLING THEME:

What is this story about? What are you saying? What idea is being explored and revealed?

Raiders of the Lost Ark: *Respect for the supernatural*

Good Will Hunting: *Embrace your true self*

The Silence of the Lambs: *Transformation and Gender*

Million Dollar Baby: *Second Chances*

Meet The Parents: *Trust*

6) CENTRAL DRAMATIC QUESTION:

The main question the story seeks to answer; the central mystery; often the same as the External Goal

Raiders of the Lost Ark: *Can Indy recover the ark from the Nazi's?*

Good Will Hunting: *Will Will Hunting embrace his gifts and escape his dead-end existence?*

The Silence of the Lambs: *Can Clarice convince Lecter to help her catch Buffalo Bill?*

Million Dollar Baby: *Can Frankie train Maggie into a champion?*

Meet The Parents: *Will Greg gain Jack's trust and ask Pam to marry him?*

7) ENDING:

How the story comes to a climax and the resolution that follows

>Raiders of the Lost Ark: *The ark is opened and Indy closes his eyes, out of respect for the supernatural power of the ark, saving himself and Marion.*
>
>Good Will Hunting: *Will leaves to find Skylar and start a new life in California.*
>
>The Silence of the Lambs: *Clarice catches Buffalo Bill on her own.*
>
>Million Dollar Baby: *Frankie makes the heart-wrenching decision to take Maggie off life support.*
>
>Meet The Parents: *Greg passes Jack's lie-detector test and proposes to Pam.*

8) ARC:

The change your protagonist goes through (or powerful realization they come to) from start to finish of the story

>*Indiana Jones: Indy goes from a lone, jaded atheist to a loving boyfriend and believer.*
>
>*Will Hunting: Will goes from an angry, violent genius trying hard to maintain his thick, emotional armor to forgiving himself and moving on with his life.*
>
>*Clarice Starling: Clarice goes from a trainee to a Federal Agent.*
>
>*Frankie Dunn: Frankie goes from a failed father and trainer to a loving father and trainer making the ultimate sacrifice for his adopted daughter, Maggie.*
>
>*Greg Focker: Greg goes from being subordinate to Jack to being his respected son-in-law.*

FROM THE TRENCHES:

THE SIXTH SENSE AND JOE ROTH

Back in the day, I wrote coverage on the submission draft of *The Sixth Sense* by M. Night Shyamalan the night before it sold in a $3 million+ deal. I was very impressed with the script, but it was a strange mix of family drama and gory horror. This draft was also too long, coming in at 126 pages. My employer didn't end up buying it, but their parent company, Disney, headed by Joe Roth, did.

My notes made two key suggestions...

- Trim! Needs cutting, especially subplots like the old man.

- Too gory. Needs to find the right balance of horror and drama.

The finished film came in at 100 minutes, the old man subplot was gone and the gore was dialed down. They had implemented all of my suggestions. (They must have read my coverage, right? That's the only explanation!)

Years later, I met Joe Roth, who greenlit the film. He confirmed that they chose to shoot the entire spec draft, rather than trim the script before production, but it became apparent in the editing room that certain scenes needed to go. They also made it more palatable for a broad audience, taking it from an expected R rating to a PG-13.

The moral of the story is twofold:

1. **Listen to your readers!** You can't ignore every note you get, especially when there's a consensus.

2. **Get it right the first time!** What's not working on the page won't work later on the screen. Trim it now and save millions! You can keep it lean, mean and focused by utilizing the powerful tool known as...

VI.   THE "FULL" STORY MAP

The Full Story Map is the addition of your plot to the Basic Story Map. You will write four Story Engines, 10 major "beats" and a complete Scene List to finish the Full Story Map in preparation of writing properly-formatted screenplay pages.

The Full Story Map is the complete meta-structure of your screenplay and the importance of it cannot be overemphasized. If Theme is the WHY you tell the story, Structure is HOW you tell it. Structure needs to be strong, and there is a definite benchmark for it.

About 95% of movies fall into a Classical Three-Act Restorative Structure. In very simple terms, Beginning, Middle, End, or Setup, Conflict, Resolution. These principles were first written about by Aristotle in approximately 350 B.C., and they have stood the test of time. I won't bother to go into more detail about the origin of this dramatic structure – there are other books that detail this fascinating lineage – all that matters now is that this is undeniably the accepted form used today in most films. It's a proven, effective way to tell a story, and all of us unconsciously look for this structuring in the films and TV shows we watch.

Restorative means that the story reaches a restoration of order by the end of the tale. An order is established at the beginning, that order is thrown into chaos, a struggle ensues in which a person makes decisions in response to conflict, and eventually a new restoration of order is established.

Even after years of study, I can't succinctly say *why* this structure works. It just does. There can be no doubt if you just watch several commercial feature films and compare their plot structure to the Full Story Map. I believe you're going to find that most of your favorite movies...every top box-office winner...every Oscar nominated film...most independent movies with name actors...yep, they all have the same basic structure of story beats with an uncannily similar placement in the running time of the movie.

Since this form is so classic and proven, it stands to reason that your screenplay should reflect this structure.

It is interesting to note that even when a screenplay for a produced film is not written exactly to these page points, the resulting FILM IS CUT to these exact specifications (substituting minutes for pages, using the *one page = one minute of screen time* rule).

An example of where these signpost beats fall in a movie (by minutes) and in a script (by pages) would be on minute/page: 1, 10, 20, 27, 40, 45, 55, 60, 75, 87, 100, 108. I've seen countless movies and read countless scripts with major beats that fall on or in extremely close range of these minutes/pages.

I already mentioned the example of how the screenplay for *The Sixth Sense* was cut down by 30 pages/minutes. *Juno* is another example. The script for *Juno* that I reference in this book was sent out to members of the Academy for Oscar consideration – it's clear that it's been trimmed to reflect the film, as there are several markers in the script for "Omitted Scene," meaning that the original script was longer. The "fat" in the script was either cut before production or was shot and left on the cutting room floor.

You may look at these examples and ask "So why can't I write a longer script as they'll expect to make cuts?" My opinion is that new writers can't afford to over-write. Your script must be tight, and it must feel exactly like a movie that could play in the theaters this weekend. That means a lean, 100-110 page, fast-paced sample of confident storytelling.

THREE ACTS = FOUR ACTS

Not to confuse you, but I separate the second act into two parts so it actually becomes a FOUR-ACT STRUCTURE.

The Midpoint beat (dead center in your script) is so crucial that it separates the second act into two distinct halves that we'll call Act Two-A and Act Two-B. You've probably heard of the dreaded term "Act Two problems," or perhaps you've heard the maxim "Act Two is where screenwriters go to die" (I might have made that one up, can't remember). This is primarily because it's so *longgggg* that it's easy to lose momentum if you don't have strong story engines and signpost beats. It's much easier to work with if you break it down into two halves.

Let's look at the functions and progression of the four basic acts from a big-picture perspective:

ACT ONE establishes the <u>order</u>, the <u>protagonist</u>, the major <u>theme</u> and the protagonist's <u>goal(s)</u>. A major <u>dramatic conflict</u> throws the order into chaos and threatens the goal, and he/she meets a <u>dynamic character</u> to escalate conflict and take them on a journey which appears to have serious consequences. An unforeseen event creates a <u>turn</u> in direction on the protagonist's journey, and they must make a <u>decision</u> in the face of increased stakes to embark on this <u>new journey</u>. The <u>antagonist</u> is introduced.

ACT TWO-A: The protagonist <u>takes control</u> in pursuit of his/her clearly defined goal in opposition of the antagonist, acting against conflict. Protagonist makes allies and overcomes trials. A <u>disaster</u> occurs and things start to <u>fall apart</u> and their plan unravels as a <u>new line of action</u> is introduced that will push them and us to the climax of the story.

ACT TWO-B: More trials and tribulation as <u>conflict escalates</u>, the dramatic landscape expands and the protagonist unleashes a campaign based on their sense of personal power. But any success is short-lived and they <u>hit bottom</u> as they are faced with the <u>consequences</u> of their decision made at the end of Act One and the Antagonist gains the upper hand. The protagonist must make a <u>decision</u> in the face of the highest conflict yet. They generally decide to <u>risk all</u> to achieve their goal with a <u>new plan</u>.

ACT THREE: The protagonist formulates the <u>method of defeat</u> to win the <u>final struggle</u> against the antagonist that sees the <u>convergence</u> of all plotlines and characters into one exciting and <u>unpredictable climax that is the ultimate expression of the theme</u>. The protagonist achieves their <u>goal(s)</u> as <u>resolution</u>, and <u>restoration</u> of a new order, are reached.

These broad strokes can apply to any genre of movie.

Sometimes the acts are easily identified by LOCATION. For example, in *Back to the Future*, the second act finds Marty McFly stuck in the 1950s. In *Star Wars* Luke Skywalker heads off on an adventure into space for act two. In *The Wizard Of Oz* Dorothy journeys into Oz for the second act, and the third act finds her in the witch's dark castle. Or in *Speed*, the three Acts are basically: bomb in the building, bomb on the bus, bomb on the subway. Simple. Keep in mind that structure may be simple, but the story need not be.

Again, this is not formula; it is <u>form</u>. You can still tell a unique, fresh story with dynamic characters within this form. It doesn't mean your story and characters have to be predictable, because ultimately it is your individual decisions that make a great story, not the form in which it is presented.

I believe strongly that you must know this blueprint before you can modify it and experiment with it, in the same way that you must understand basic engineering principles before you can design a motor on an advanced computer design system. A famous screenwriting guru tells us there are three basic story forms for screenplays: Classical, Minimalist, and Anti-Structure. However, the latter two are not independent of the Classical form; they merely *modify* it; thus a screenwriter must learn and master the Classical design before embarking on the other two variations.

From being audience members for most of our lives, all of us have an inherent sense of this structure, which is why, for example, we naturally sense something is wrong if we're watching a movie and the main story has not been introduced by the thirty minute mark. (It also applies to novels, in which if nothing major happens by page 100 - 130, we might feel the story is moving too slowly.)

STORY ENGINES

A Story Engine is a plot device that drives the story for a certain length of time. Some might call them "mini-movies" or "mini-goals," or you may just want to think of a Story Engine as a <u>Line of Action</u>: a character taking active steps toward a goal.

I suggest you define a clear Story Engine for each of the four acts so you and the reader know where the story is headed as you create expectations – then it's your job as the writer to *subvert* those expectations and surprise the reader with shocking turns. You're planting setups and detonating payoffs.

In the submarine thriller *U-571*, the American crew must capture the German sub, pilot it home when their own sub is destroyed, then take out a German super destroyer (with no power and only one torpedo). These sections of the story are very clearly delineated and driven by escalating conflict.

Think of your story in four sections; then try to reduce each section to one line of action – like a "mini-logline" for each act. The best way to define a Story Engine is to answer the question, "What does the protagonist <u>have to do</u> in this chapter of the story?"

Here's an example of a well-known film in four sections,
Aliens:

- *One*: RIPLEY must join a platoon of gung-ho Marines
  to investigate a deserted colony that may have been
  attacked by the aliens that almost killed her.

- *Two-A*: Ripley fights alongside the Marines, and
  protects the child NEWT from the aliens as they are
  surrounded and stranded on the planet.

- *Two-B*: As they take more casualties, Ripley struggles
  to stay alive and get to the escape ship, but Newt is
  captured. She decides to risk her life to go back and
  find Newt.

- *Three*: Ripley rescues Newt from the Alien Queen's
  nest and must battle the Alien Queen on the landing
  platform, defeating her.

Notice how Ripley is in defensive mode until the end of Act
Two, when she decides to risk all to mount an offensive
against the villain. This actively pushes her and us into the
final race to the climax, which becomes the most satisfying
kind of ending for the reader and audience: a direct
confrontation between protagonist and antagonist. Also
notice how strong, active verbs are used to describe her
actions: *investigate, fight, struggles, risk her life, find,
rescues, battle*. You don't want the actions in your Story
Engines to be verbs like *thinks, discusses, replies*. Show,
don't Tell!

One tendency in defining an Act Two-B engine can be to
describe the "hitting bottom" without defining the
protagonist's pursuit of their goal to get there. For example,
in *Aliens*, the Act Two-B engine is not "Newt is captured;"
it's what Ripley must do before she fails and Newt is
captured (hitting bottom at the end of Act Two), because
this is the line of action that we follow as conflict escalates
and Ripley's fortunes go south.

We'll look at the above engines for *Aliens* from a different perspective in the Theme chapter.

Think of a Story Engine as the machine behind your main character's quest — it's what gives momentum and urgency to the story.

Television gives us a clear way of looking at Story Engines. There's a practical reason why there's so many cop shows, medical shows and legal shows: the writers are never starved for a story. It's always organic to introduce a new crime, a new patient or a new trial.

J.J. Abrams cites the inspiration for his spy show *Alias* as a joke he made to his fellow writers when they were struggling to come up with stories for the college student protagonist in *Felicity*: Abrams quipped, "This would be a lot easier if Felicity was a super spy."

One can imagine that "a drama about relationships" is tougher to plot than "a spy thriller about a nuclear bomb hijacked by a terrorist." In either case, make it easier on yourself and more compelling for the reader by defining a main thrust for each act.

A Story Engine can also act as a framing device, like bookends, that fuels the story or takes us into it.

A famous example: *Citizen Kane* uses the framing device of a reporter's investigation, thus motivating a trip through the life of Charles Foster Kane, all in answer to the question, "What is Rosebud?"

In the HBO drama *Six Feet Under*, each episode opens with a death. The corpse is brought into the mortuary which is owned and operated by our main characters, the Fisher family, and we are ushered into their new set of personal struggles.

Six Feet Under lasted five seasons — as the first episode of the series opened with the death of the Fisher family's patriarch, they ended the series with an incredible flash-forward montage of the deaths of all the main characters. It made for bitter-sweet bookends.

Here are some sample engines:

The Hangover STORY ENGINES:

ACT 1: The guys go to Las Vegas and kick off the night with a toast.

ACT 2A: The guys follow their initial clues to find Doug.

ACT 2B: The guys must return Mike Tyson's tiger and bring Mr. Chao his money to find Doug.

ACT 3: The race home, the wedding goes off well and Stu dumps Melissa.

Gladiator STORY ENGINES:

ACT 1: Maximus struggles to retire from war and go home, but Commodus leads a coup and kills his family.

ACT 2A: Maximus must survive slavery and gladiator battles in Northern Africa.

ACT 2B: Maximus must survive in Rome, become a great gladiator ("win the crowd") and get close to Commodus.

ACT 3: Maximus must kill Commodus.

As Good As It Gets STORY ENGINES:

ACT 1: Melvin attempts to preserve his isolated world but is challenged by his gay neighbor and his sassy waitress.

ACT 2A: Melvin must take care of Simon's dog and get Carol back to work.

ACT 2B: Melvin must win Simon and Carol's trust as they bond, leaving him alone.

ACT 3: Melvin must truly care for Simon and Carol to gain happiness.

META-STRUCTURE OR "THE WAY INTO THE STORY"

I'd suggest that you think about the general way that you're going to tell the story before you start to lay out your beat sheet and scene list. What's your way into this story? How are you going to approach the writing of your buddy-cop action movie so it's a fresh take on this proven genre rather than another tired entry?

Up tells a story of an old man who's clinging to the past. He goes on a journey to recover his youth, but his true mission is to help a boy who's held back by his own personal history. The villain of the story is a man who was our protagonist's boyhood hero.

The Usual Suspects is literally told to us by Kevin Spacey's character, who spins a long-winded tale meant to answer the question, "Who is Keyser Soze?" The answer is not revealed until the very end when we learn that *he* is Keyser Soze.

Slumdog Millionaire uses the questions in the quiz show as catalysts for flashbacks that show us the life of Jamal, the protagonist, and how he gathered the information to answer the questions.

The pilot for the TV drama *Sons of Anarchy* contains some very familiar elements; it's *Hamlet* in a biker gang.

These examples were the screenwriters' "way in" to telling the story. They chose these narrative devices because they best exemplified the elements in their Basic Story Map.

Many movies or TV shows begin with the ending and the screenwriter *reverse-engineers* the story from there. They build events that organically lead up to this climax.

The germ of *Little Miss Sunshine* was that Michael Arndt was watching a child beauty pageant, and he thought about what would happen if an awkward girl got up on stage and "just started kicking ass." The resulting script is a series of scenes in a classical structure that push to the hilarious climax that finds young Olive dancing to Rick James' *Superfreak* for her entry in the talent competition...and then her family joins her on stage and they *all* start dancing like maniacs. Incidentally, this climax also represents the ultimate fruition of the theme, which is "we are all freaks." The movie is also explicitly about *competition*, thus each character is in some way involved in a contest to be the best in their chosen field.

The pilot for the brilliant TV drama *Mad Men* shows us Don Draper, a Manhattan ad exec and dashing playboy who drinks, smokes and meets his girlfriend for a noon-time romp during his lunch break. He flirts with every woman and they flirt back, while gossiping about this legendary cocksman. The very last scene shows him pulling up to his suburban home, walking into the house and saying goodnight...to his wife and kids.

Once you know your Meta-Structure—how you're going to begin and end the story and the perspective that the audience will see it from—you want to think of your story as a series of...

LINES OF ACTION

A line of action is simply a character pursuing a goal. You want to have multiple lines of action to flesh out your story and your characters, at the least, two, which ideally would be the External and Internal Goals of the protagonist.

Notice in the sample Story Maps how I've defined two separate points for some of the signpost beats. For example, you might see the Inciting Incident (External) on page 8 and the Inciting Incident (Internal) on page 10. It depends on the story.

It helps to categorize your lines of action as the *A, B* or *C* story so you can prioritize their page count in the script. E.g.,

A story = Protagonist's External line

B story = Protagonist's Internal line

C story = Antagonist's or Dynamic Character's line

For example, in *Sideways*, the three lines of action are built on relationships:

A story = Miles (Paul Giamatti) and Jack (Thomas Haden Church)

B story = Miles and Maya (Virginia Madsen)

C story = Jack and Stephanie (Sandra Oh)

You may want to add subplots to make for some dynamic payoffs and to add arcs to your supporting characters. The key is to show these characters progressing by taking action.

You may have a subplot shown in flashback – if so, the flashbacks must advance the present line of action, as well. A flashback is inherently inactive since it takes place in the past, so the way to make it active is to make sure that it is crucial and it escalates the conflict and stakes. If a flashback is not causing <u>change</u> – either an advancement of the present story line or a new understanding of the present story line – then it is *not* crucial and it should be cut.

As Good As It Gets is a nice example of multiple lines of action – one could look at it as a multi-protagonist story, since Jack Nicholson, Helen Hunt and Greg Kinnear all have separate goals and sources of conflict, although it is still anchored with a *main* protagonist, Jack Nicholson's Melvin Udall. Melvin needs to learn how to love while Carol needs to help her sick son and Simon needs to get back the money he lost after he was attacked and hospitalized.

In *Little Miss Sunshine*, there are several lines of action for the family members: Greg Kinnear tries to sell his personal development system. Paul Dano tries to maintain his vow of silence so he can realize his dream of becoming a fighter pilot. Steve Carell must get over the break-up that led to his recent suicide attempt. Toni Collette is just trying to hold her family together and little Abigail Breslin competes to win the titular child beauty pageant. (The hilarious grandfather, played by Alan Arkin, does not have an actual arc, but he provides a skewed "voice of reason," acts as commentary on and a foil to various characters and sets up the outrageous dance scene finale.) One could make up a Full Story Map for each one of these characters or just define their steps in the scene list; it's up to you.

I've found it helpful at times to construct a linear grid with each character having their own line and noting their beats along their lines, with eventual convergence in Act Three.

Here's a linear grid built on a hypothetical story in which the External line is launched in the Opening, the Internal line begins at the Inciting Incident and the "C" story begins at Strong Movement Forward.

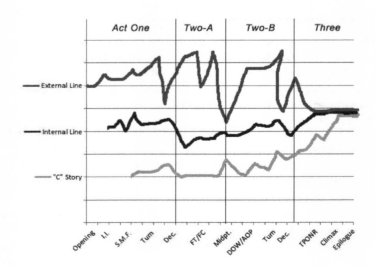

The dips and peaks of the lines can represent escalating conflict, turns in direction or just serve as visual markers for the signpost beats.

Note how the External and Internal lines converge at the True Point of No Return to create one, driving line to push to the Climax, the point at which the character driving the "C" story catches up to them and joins in the final battle. (Convergence at the end of Act Two is also a common device.)

Another example from television: the classic sitcom *Seinfeld*. In the best episodes, there are four separate lines of action, all linked to the goals of the main characters. For example in "The Frogger:"

- George must get the Frogger video game out of the pizza shop without turning off the power so as to preserve his high score.

- Kramer must investigate the Riverside Park killer known as "The Lopper" so as to warn Jerry how to avoid the killer.

- Jerry must dump his new girlfriend, the "sentence finisher," because she lives near the park where The Lopper is beheading his victims, but she won't let him finish his break-up speech.

- Elaine must replace her boss' vintage cake that came from the court of King Edward VI with an Entenmann's cake, hoping he won't notice.

Newman!

CLASSICAL FOUR-ACT STRUCTURE STEPS OR "STORY BEATS"

It's time for that all-important "Beat Sheet" that all the cool kids are talking about.

There is a very clear and familiar plot progression to most screenplays that is recognized and understood by every professional Reader in the film industry. A new writer must structure their script exactly to this tried-and-true paradigm of Classical screenplay structure. It is my opinion that you must first master this structure before attempting to subvert it. You must get it right down to the page. Readers look for this. The pros use it. It is undoubtedly the "industry standard."

You must balance your story to the four acts. Each act represents *roughly* 25% of the total length of your story (I say roughly because as we will see, the actual lengths of each act in the modern, 110-page screenplay are not equally 25% as they may have been in a Syd Field-era 120 pager.) Here are the four acts in very broad strokes:

ACT ONE: The Crisis & The Decision

ACT TWO-A: Protagonist takes action

ACT TWO-B: Things fall apart

ACT THREE: The Final Struggle & The Resolution

Classical Four-Act Structure can be broken down into ten main plot steps or *beats* (the 11th, EPILOGUE, and two sub-beats, COMBAT and ONE HOUR WAR, are optional). These events form the "tentpoles" of your narrative structure. My beat sheet is based on a 110-page screenplay, which I suggest as your target length; the corresponding page numbers for each step are given.

Note: This is *not* a complete scene list (you'll get to that after you compile your Full Story Map and before you start writing screenplay pages), just the major moments – the BIG events – that drive the story. It is very important that these plot points occur in the proper page range.

In this section, we will look at each beat's general characteristics in an ordered list; then I will provide a more focused look with examples from well-known movies.

ACT ONE:

1) **OPENING** (page 1-3): Establishes ORDER (the unique world of the story) and the PROTAGONIST and communicates the THEME. (Ideally, it can also establish the protagonist's GOALS and introduce the CENTRAL DRAMATIC QUESTION, but these can wait until End of Act One at the latest.)

2) **INCITING INCIDENT** (page 8-10): The first disturbance to the order that sets the story in motion. An event that brings about danger, CONFLICT and chaos. Introduces the MAIN DRAMATIC CONFLICT and maybe the ANTAGONIST.

3) **STRONG MOVEMENT FORWARD** (page 17-20): The protagonist truly takes their "first step" on their "core journey," whether voluntary or not. The protagonist is inspired, swept away or given a strong push toward their External Goal. This movement may come in the form of a revelation or the introduction of the DYNAMIC CHARACTER or MENTOR who beckons our protagonist on this journey.

4) **END OF ACT ONE EVENT/TURN & DECISION** (page 25-30): An unforeseen EVENT causes great conflict and a TURN in direction of the story (usually, a turn on the External line of action), and the protagonist makes an active DECISION in the face of this conflict and chooses a path, entering a gateway – the story is propelled into Act Two in a new direction and very often a CHANGE IN LOCATION. The protagonist formulates their first major plan of action that they will follow for Act 2A. External Goal, Internal Goal, Central Dramatic Question and the Act Two-A Story Engine must be established by end of Act One, ideally by page 30.

Remember: TURN *and* DECISION.

Take note: A perfect 30 page Act One is golden!

ACT TWO-A

5) **FIRST TRIAL/FIRST CASUALTY** (page 38-40): The "40-Minute Trial." The first major obstacle on the protagonist's new journey. A <u>skirmish,</u> foreshadowing a larger battle, that raises the stakes and reminds the protagonist of the consequences of their new commitment. The "casualty" may be the death of an ally or a figurative death; the threat has *become real.*

Note: In some instances, this beat may be *only* a casualty — e.g., a detective discovers a second dead body, which now means that the killer is a serial killer. In this case, if the protagonist is not active, then they must be active in the next sub-beat...

> 5A) **COMBAT** (optional) (page 45): The First Casualty generates a more direct confrontation. If the Trial was a skirmish, this is a BATTLE, more personal and with higher stakes.

6) **MIDPOINT** (page 50-55): A DISASTER occurring DEAD CENTER in your story that RAISES THE STAKES, threatens the goal, and PUSHES THE ACTION TO THE CLIMAX with new Story Engine(s). False goals become true goals. Foreshadows the climax and establishes a CLOCK, a time deadline, that escalates conflict and deepens consequences. (Note: if the Midpoint is seemingly a happy moment, like the first kiss between two lovers, then it must represent a disaster in the larger story by escalating conflict and setting up a future sacrifice and confrontation, e.g., the two lovers are married to other people, so this kiss is an inevitable ticket to the destruction of one or both marriages.)

> 6A) **ONE HOUR WAR/TRIUMPH** (optional) (page 60): The one hour mark is often a staple of a movie's

structure and present in many screenplays on or around page 60. I sometimes think of it as a "Big Boom!" (Note: This may act as the Midpoint but I don't suggest you wait until page 60 as modern scripts move faster and the reader is going to start looking for your Midpoint around page 50.)

ACT TWO-B

7) **DECLARATION OF WAR/ASSUMPTION OF POWER** (page 75): The protagonist experiences a surge of strength, realizes their TRUE POWER and they either initiate a direct attack on the Antagonist or they prepare/TRAINS for the inevitable showdown.

8) **END OF ACT TWO EVENT/TURN & DECISION** (page 85-90): Another major, shocking EVENT turns the story in a new direction. The dramatic landscape broadens or "opens up," as the threat worsens and perhaps takes a new form and the hero HITS BOTTOM, feeling the dire CONSEQUENCES of their decision at the end of Act One (note the link between how they dealt with the End of Act One's Event/Turn and now). Plotlines CONVERGE to focus the story and force the protagonist to make a NEW DECISION to "risk all" to achieve his/her goal, pass through a new gateway and propel themselves and us into Act Three. This also may signal another major CHANGE OF LOCATION, and it establishes the Act Three Story Engine to push to the Climax.

Note: This may see the culmination of one or two lines of action, e.g., the protagonist may win over their love interest here to achieve their Internal Goal, as long as the External Goal is still in jeopardy for the final act.

Again: TURN *and* DECISION.

Note: Ending your Act Two on page 90 is golden!

ACT THREE

9) **TRUE POINT OF NO RETURN** (page 98-100): A deadly ESCALATION that conclusively sets up the final battle; ratchets the stakes and tension up another notch as the threat takes on even more power, becoming seemingly insurmountable. The protagonist makes a statement of intentions and/or finds the antagonist's Achilles Heel, formulating the method of defeat. From this point on, there truly is NO RETURN! If they did not truly risk everything at the End of Act Two, then they must do so here. They go "all in," so to speak.

10) **CLIMAX** (page 105-110): The FINAL DIRECT CONFRONTATION between protagonist and antagonist that brings together all plot threads while representing the ultimate expression of the theme and resulting in a NEW RESTORATION OF ORDER. (Note: The protagonist almost always must act alone to deliver the final blow that will defeat the antagonist and achieve the external goal.)

11) **EPILOGUE** (optional): Shows the NEW ORDER (without *explaining* it) and the final resolution.

And that's it! The beauty of these beats is that they are more specific than any other template I've found, yet they are broad enough for you to have complete creative control of how to utilize the structure and satisfy the characteristics.

BUILDING A BETTER HERO

I've intentionally named these beats with titles that do not commit too much to a certain type or tone. For example, I've never liked certain beats in the Hero's Journey such as "Approach to the Inmost Cave" or "The Seizing of the Sword." Those descriptions come across as limiting to me and make me think only of Fantasy or Science Fiction, certainly not a contemporary drama or workplace comedy. In other screenwriting books, I've seen too-broad terms like

"Pinch" to represent what I call the First Trial/First Casualty and the Declaration of War/Assumption of Power.

I also don't see the need to differentiate between a *need*, a *goal* and a *desire* if they all mean the same thing!

The Story Map beat sheet is an emotional map that applies to any type of movie story — it is *not* a genre-specific template.

As I've said before, I don't see the value in mere categorization for the sake of it. It doesn't help you to put every character into a category, such as Trickster, Herald or Threshold Guardian, unless these types are fixed to a specific beat and page range in which their functions are crucial.

THE POWER OF TWO

Keep in mind that the protagonist's pursuit of their External and Internal goals are two separate lines of action, thus, it may make sense for you to define two beats at some or all of the signpost positions on your beat sheet. See the *Juno* beat sheet below for an example of this technique.

FIRST SAMPLE BEAT SHEET: *JUNO*

The plot structure of *Juno,* written by Diablo Cody, adheres perfectly to the beat sheet in the Full Story Map. Note that this map is based on the screenplay, not the film. The numbers represent the page that the beat occurs (if there's a range given, it means the execution of this plot movement was spread over two pages).

Take note how closely the script adheres to the Story Map page ranges: Act One ends on page 30...Act Two ends on 90...and there are major beats at 10, 20, 27, 40, 55, 75, 87, and 100.

Below is the beat sheet. As a reminder, here are Juno's goals:

EXTERNAL GOAL: To have the baby and give it to the Lorings.

INTERNAL GOAL: To get together with Paulie.

JUNO

Screenplay written by Diablo Cody

101 pages

BEAT SHEET

(note: this is not a complete scene list, only a list of the major "signpost" plot points)

ACT ONE

1-4 – **OPENING:** JUNO (Ellen Page) takes her third pregnancy test - it still says she's pregnant.

9-10 – **INCITING INCIDENT:** Juno tells Paulie Bleeker (Michael Cera) she's pregnant and she plans to get an abortion.

20 – **STRONG MOVEMENT FORWARD:** Juno flees the abortion clinic.

26 – **END OF ACT ONE TURN (EXTERNAL):** Juno tells her father MAC (J.K. Simmons) and stepmom BREN (Allison Janney) that she's pregnant.

27 – **END OF ACT ONE TURN (INTERNAL):** Juno tells them that Bleeker is the father—they break out in laughter!

29 – **END OF ACT ONE DECISION (EXTERNAL & INTERNAL):** Juno agrees to let her Dad take her to meet the Lorings, the adoptive couple she found in the Penny Saver.

30 – ACT I ends.

ACT TWO-A

40 – FIRST TRIAL/FIRST CASUALTY: Mark (Jason Bateman) and Juno make a connection over music, drawing Vanessa's (Jennifer Garner) concern.

55 – MIDPOINT: Vanessa walks in on Mark and Juno alone in the house; Vanessa is suspicious, but she relaxes when she sees the ultrasound.

60 – WAR: Juno fights with her stepmom Bren when Bren tells her not to visit Mark, a married man.

ACT TWO-B

75 – DOW/AOP (INTERNAL): Juno has a big fight with Bleeker because he's taking another girl to the prom; this is the first time she's actually showing that she has real feelings for him, but she won't admit it.

77 – DOW/AOP (EXTERNAL): Angry, Juno drives back to Mark's house.

85 – END OF ACT TWO TURN (EXTERNAL): Mark tells Vanessa that he wants out of their marriage and the adoption.

87 – END OF ACT TWO DECISION (EXTERNAL): Juno leaves note for Vanessa (we don't know what's in it yet.)

88 – END OF ACT TWO TURN (INTERNAL): Juno goes to her dad in despair about couples and love. He tells her that the one for her is the guy who will always love her, unconditionally.

90 – END OF ACT TWO DECISION (INTERNAL): Juno realizes that Paulie is the one - she leaves to find him.

ACT THREE

94 – TRUE POINT OF NO RETURN: Juno kisses Paulie and soon after, at home, her water breaks. Her dad rushes her to the hospital as Paulie runs in his track meet.

98 – CLIMAX (INTERNAL): Paulie joins her at the hospital after she's given birth; she cries in his arms, as they deal with the loss of the baby *together*.

99 – CLIMAX (EXTERNAL): Vanessa cares for her baby at home. She has framed Juno's letter which says, "Vanessa – if you're still in, I'm still in. Juno."

100 - 101 EPILOGUE: Juno and her official boyfriend, Paulie, who is "totally boss as far as boyfriends go," sing a song together.

You'll note that the Act Three beats fall a bit sooner than my paradigm, due to the shorter length of this script (101 pages vs. 110 pages in the paradigm). This is perfectly acceptable, although I suggest you adhere to the paradigm locations up until roughly page 90 when Act Three begins. As you'll see with a number of modern films, Act Three can be quite short: in *Juno*, it's only 10 pages.

Note: a more detailed map of *Juno* is available in the companion book, *Story Maps: Booster Pack #1.*

SECOND SAMPLE BEAT SHEET: *HUSTLE & FLOW*

Hustle & Flow, written and directed by Craig Brewer, is a gritty and inspiring music drama that adheres exactly to the Story Map.

Act One ends at minute 30...Act Two ends at 90...the major beats occur at 10, 20, 27, 55, 75, 87, 100 and 107. Sound familiar?

Hustle & Flow's story is focused on one throughline (more so than *Juno*) so I don't see the need to break out External and Internal beats.

HUSTLE & FLOW
Independent Music Drama
Written and Directed by Craig Brewer
110 minutes

BEAT SHEET

(note: this is not a complete scene list)

ACT ONE

1 – **OPENING:** DJay, a poor pimp and weed dealer in Memphis, gives one of his hustles, a speech that he'll reference throughout the story that states the theme: "What do you want to do with your life?"

6 – ARNEL asks DJay to bring his best weed for famous rapper Skinny Black to his July 4th party.

10 – **INCITING INCIDENT:** Djay buys a keyboard from a crackhead, starts playing music.

20 – **STRONG MOVEMENT FORWARD:** Djay watches his old friend KEY record a singer in church. Djay is deeply affected, cries.

27 – END OF ACT ONE TURN: Djay shows up at Key's home in the suburbs to recruit him for the band. Tension is high because Djay has brought two of his hos and Key's wife Yvette is a conservative woman.

28 – END OF ACT ONE DECISION: Djay pulls out his keyboard to audition his raps for Key. Key joins in.

30 – Key joins the crew, ending Act One.

ACT TWO-A

40 – FIRST TRIAL: Djay and his crew record their first song: "Whoop that Trick."

45 – FIRST CASUALTY: A troubled Key tells Djay he needs the music to be successful or he will feel like a failure to his wife.

46 – COMBAT: Djay fights with Lexus, kicks her and her baby out of the house after she belittles him about his dream of being a rapper.

55 – MIDPOINT: After a big fight with the guys, Djay recruits Shug to sing on his song, "It's Hard Out Here for a Pimp." Although it's tense, they bond, leading to their inevitable union.

60 – TRIUMPH: The song turns out amazing and Shug is elated.

ACT TWO-B

75 – DOW/AOP: Djay sings his final song, "Keep Hustlin'," his most personal and accomplished yet, as he prepares to meet Skinny Black. He's ready to make his final move to capture his dream.

87 – END OF ACT TWO TURN: Djay's first attempt to hustle Skinny Black fails; he hits bottom.

88 – END OF ACT TWO DECISION: Djay RISKS ALL to confront Skinny Black with an aggressive, brilliant hustle.

90 – It works. Djay hooks Skinny Black, ending Act Two.

ACT THREE

100 – TRUE POINT OF NO RETURN: Djay gets in a shootout and is chased out of the club.

107 – CLIMAX: Djay's song "Whoop That Trick" becomes a hit song!

110 – EPILOGUE: Two prison guards give Djay their demo tape. He's now the star that others are trying to hustle. He says: "You know what they say? Everybody got to have a dream."

Note: a more detailed map of *Hustle & Flow* is available in the companion book, *Story Maps: Booster Pack #1*.

THIRD SAMPLE BEAT SHEET: *UP*

Pixar's *Up* is a fine example of the mini-studio's ability to produce touching stories for broad audiences— they are masters at creating the coveted "four quadrant" films that Hollywood salivates over, meaning they appeal to male and female kids and male and female adults.

Although *Up* has some stilted dialogue and cliché moments, it features some fantastic thematic work, thrilling set pieces and powerful character arcs. Note: The length is short – only 89 minutes – so the beats that follow the *Declaration of War/Assumption of Power* occur sooner than with a longer script.

Up
Animated Action-Comedy
Screenplay by Bob Peterson & Pete Docter
89 Minutes

BEAT SHEET

(note: this is not a complete scene list)

ACT ONE

1 – **OPENING:** Montage of CARL and his wife ELLIE over the years. They lost a baby.

10 – **INCITING INCIDENT:** Carl buys tickets for Paradise Falls and Ellie dies before they can go.

20 – **STRONG MOVEMENT FORWARD:** Carl launches his house into the air, and discovers RUSSELL is his stowaway.

27 – **END OF ACT ONE TURN**: Carl and Russell hit a dangerous storm.

30 – **END OF ACT ONE DECISION**: Carl guides the house to a crash landing near Paradise Falls.

ACT TWO-A

40 – **FIRST TRIAL/FIRST CASUALTY**: Carl gets talked into taking KEVIN, the bird, and DUG, the dog, with them, which complicates their journey to the falls.

45 – **COMBAT**: They are hunted by the evil dogs.

53–55 – **MIDPOINT**: They meet the famous adventurer CHARLES MUNTZ, Carl's childhood hero, and learn he is evil and has been hunting Kevin for years. Carl and Russell must save Kevin and escape Muntz' dirigible, protected by his dark army of scary dogs.

ACT TWO-B

60 – **WAR**: They run for their lives!

75 – **DECLARATION OF WAR/ASSUMPTION OF POWER**: Carl throws his old possessions out of his house and takes flight, leaving behind the old Carl and declaring war on Muntz to save his adopted child, Russell, and Kevin.

80 – **END OF ACT TWO TURN**: All sides battle. Carl vs. Muntz. Dug vs. the Doberman. Russell vs. the dogs.

DECISION: Carl puts his plan to defeat Muntz into action.

ACT THREE

85 – **TRUE POINT OF NO RETURN**: Carl cleverly defeats Muntz. As Muntz falls to his death, Carl loses the house in the clouds. Carl: "You know, it's just a house." He's decided to live in this life, not in the past.

86 – Kevin, revealed to be a girl, gives birth to chicks!

87 – **CLIMAX**: Carl and Russell pilot Muntz's blimp home, and Carl stands in as Russell's father when Russell receives his Boy Scouts badge for "Assisting the Elderly." Carl gives him "Ellie's Badge."

89 – EPILOGUE: Carl and Russell eat ice cream and the final image shows the house on Paradise Falls. Carl's dream has been achieved. The End.

Note: a more detailed map of *Up* is available in the companion book, *Story Maps: Booster Pack #1*.

FROM THE TRENCHES:

JEFFREY REDDICK
(creator of the *Final Destination* franchise)

"Studios look at theatrical these days as mostly PR for the DVD release."

Prints and Advertising costs for a theatrical release are so expensive that it's smarter to send more films straight to video, even when they feature major stars. In this sense, theatrical release is the pie in the sky, so don't make it your only goal.

The Lesson: Compartmentalize your goals into more practical, shorter-term milestones: get your script read by decision-makers...write a short film and find filmmakers to shoot it...get a meeting...a manager...an option...get in the guild, etc.

These goals can happen in different orders. There are no hard and fast rules to how you get there. Make your own path.

VII.   THEME

We touched on theme a bit earlier when discussing the Basic and Full Story Map, but it should be discussed more at length since it is such a powerful tool to help give focus, cohesion and resonance to your screenplay.

Some writers start with Theme, developing the story from an idea or moral that they wish to explore. Others map out a basic story, look at it and determine what they're trying to say or what theme these elements would most logically express.

Theme can be your way into a story. For example, Danny Boyle and Simon Beaufoy made two films based on real-life scenarios, *Slumdog Millionaire* and *127 Hours* – in both they found the way into the story by exploring a core theme and designing scenes around it, some true to life and others fictional: "destiny" in *Slumdog Millionaire* and "perseverance" in *127 Hours*.

With *The Social Network*, Aaron Sorkin looked at the life of Facebook founder Mark Zuckerberg and decided that he would tell a story about status – here was a guy who was constantly trying to raise his status, to be seen as something greater or cooler than he was. Sorkin decided to inject some irony into the story by portraying the inventor of a popular social network as a socially awkward guy.

Sideways is about aging on many levels, the first one being the aging of wine. The older wine gets, the more it improves, but only to a point when it peaks. It must reach the proper level of maturity to realize its true power. Miles Raymond is a failed novelist and failed husband who has given up on life. His buddy Jack still acts like he's a frat boy.

Please Give by writer/director Nicole Holofcener is also about aging. The story is constructed around situations and characters that all have to do with aging, time and the generation gap. The central husband and wife couple in the story is waiting for the old woman next door to die so they can claim her condo. The old woman's granddaughter is a 30-something chanteuse who is obsessed with the younger woman that her boyfriend dumped her for. The husband makes his move on her and they have an affair. Meanwhile, the couple's young daughter is dealing with the typical high school dilemmas of a teenage girl.

Aliens is a great example of how the meta-structure of a story is completely derived from theme. Who would have thought that a bad-ass movie about space marines versus alien monsters would actually be about family? Here's a look at the four acts expanded from our earlier look (in Story Engines) to showcase the use of theme...

RIPLEY is an *orphan*, having been the only survivor of an attack on her colony (her adopted "family") by deadly alien monsters. She is *adopted* by a new family, albeit a dysfunctional one: a platoon of gung-ho Marines. Their mission is to save the family members of another colony on a distant moon that may have been overrun by the aliens. They get to the deserted colony, finding the only survivor is an *orphan*, a little girl named NEWT; Ripley *adopts* this girl, becoming her surrogate mother.

Their first fire fight leads to casualties to the Marine family, causing breakup of morale and solidarity. When their rescue ship crashes, the Marines are stranded on this dangerous colony, being attacked from all sides by the horde of aliens.

Ripley struggles to stay alive and defend her step-child. One by one Ripley's adopted family is killed off, and Newt is captured, certain to be killed. As their base crumbles around them and the escape ship waits, Ripley decides to go back and find Newt.

Ripley arms herself for a one-woman battle against the aliens. Ripley finds Newt in an *egg* contained in the *nest* of the massive QUEEN MOTHER. Ripley rescues Newt, burns the nest and runs from the Queen Mother to the escape craft. They escape the planet, but the Queen Mother has stowed away on the ship and attacks Ripley on the loading dock. Ripley battles the Queen Mother, mother against mother, for custody of the child. Ripley triumphs and saves Newt. The final image is of mother and child, sleeping next to one another, safe.

The Silence of the Lambs explores powerful themes of transformation and gender, reflected in the characters of Clarice Starling (Jodie Foster) and Jame Gumb, aka "Buffalo Bill" (Ted Field). Jame Gumb has hatched a murderous scheme to transform himself into a woman, and Clarice is acting against orders to rise above her trainee status and to become a woman who can stand on her own, no longer in her father's shadow and no longer the cute little girl in the room who's playing federal agent. (Her petite size is continually emphasized as she is forced to be in rooms around taller, physically stronger men.)

In *Tropic Thunder*, every character is living with some sort of false identity. Ben Stiller fakes like he cares about social causes when all he cares about is himself. Robert Downey, Jr. looks and acts like a black man, staying "in character" even when the cameras aren't rolling. Jack Black tries to cover up that he's a drug addict. Nick Nolte has lied about his military service and even fakes that he's missing a hand. The young rapper turned actor is secretly gay. The events of the story push all of these characters to crisis points where they must overcome their fear of showing their true selves to the world.

OPEN AND END ON THEME

Theme can inform every scene in your script, but when you're writing your initial Story Map, it's most crucial to express your Controlling Theme in your Opening and Climax. (I refer to it as "controlling" because the theme can literally control your characters' actions and add cohesion and direction to the plot. When you're stuck as to how a character might act in a scene, ask yourself how they might best express the theme.)

In your opening 10 pages, you want to express your Controlling Theme. Try to come up with an image or situation that encompasses the film as a whole – either your unique dramatic situation, your compelling main character, or the overriding IDEA that you are exploring/communicating.

The audience does not need to understand your theme right away; it can become clear later. An example of this is the opening of *The Dark Knight*. The Joker says "I believe whatever doesn't kill you, simply makes you…stranger." He's stating the theme: if you terrorize people with the threat of death, they will act in chaotic, self-destructive ways.

The hand in the wheat field at the opening of *Gladiator* is an image that we will later associate with Maximus ascending to heaven to join his family. But to explain it now, at the start of the narrative, would be to give away that our hero is going to die in the end. So the filmmakers leave it as a compelling, mysterious image and move on. Now, just for good measure, in the following battle scene in Germania, Maximus comes right out and states the theme of the film when he calls out a battle cry to his troops (and the audience): "What we do in this life echoes in eternity!" This expresses the theme of "the afterlife," or more specifically, man's actions on Earth and how they reflect his status in the afterlife. This theme will be discussed and explored in dialogue throughout the film. (Also, just for good measure, another key line from the opening touches on the themes of the afterlife: "On my command, unleash hell." Maximus could have said "Crush your enemies," but that wouldn't have been on theme.)

In the opening of *As Good as it Gets*, we see Jack Nicholson stuff his neighbor's dog down the trash chute. This is a very strong, unique, funny action that establishes his character, the theme (pessimism) and his main Goal: to push others away. We will later realize this is a "False Goal," but, nevertheless, it's what will drive the first Act of the film; he will constantly fight to isolate himself and maintain the status quo of his own crazy world.

Melvin Udall's final action, to kiss Carol, is preceded by his line, "I'm gonna grab ya," and he pulls her in for a kiss. He begins with pushing, ends with pulling. Not bad.

Rain Man opens on Charlie Babbit (Tom Cruise) supervising a shipment of Lamborghini sports cars, a cold symbol of raw materialism and status. It closes with him putting his brother Raymond (Dustin Hoffman) on a train, the oldest form of transportation we have, and promising him that he'll visit soon. Charlie has gone from greed to belief in family.

PREVALENT THEMES

Our popular films and tv shows tend to mine the same batch of "classic" themes. In fact, much of our classic literature and mythology expresses the same pool of themes. The reason these stories have been enjoyed all over the world for centuries is their universal appeal, which one can say is the function of art: to explore, explain and express the human condition. In Arthur Miller's words, "to make us feel less alone."

One of the most prevalent themes in all of literature and cinema that is still wildly popular was perhaps best expressed by Jesus in the New Testament:

What does it profit a man to gain the entire world but lose his soul?

Charles Foster Kane...Scrooge...Gordon Gekko...Bruce Wayne...Charlie Babbit...Howard Hughes...Mark Zuckerberg...the list goes on -- All characters in films where the spoils of their wealth were weighed against the loss of their family/friends/moral core/health.

How many times have we seen the story of the type-A workaholic who must choose between their job and their kids? (Just once I'd like to see them choose the job! Just to shake things up a bit, ya know?)

The Sixth Sense is about "family communication." It's reflected in all of the major lines of action:

- Cole is struggling to work up the courage to tell his mother about his powers.

- Malcolm is trying to get Cole to trust and open up to him.

- Malcolm is trying to get his wife to forgive him.

- The ghosts are trying to send messages to Cole, but he's too scared to realize that they need his help.

- Cole's grandmother tells Cole the message for him to pass on to his mother.

This results in Malcolm and Cole sharing the same External Goal while having their own Internal Goals:

	External Goal	Internal Goal
Malcolm Crowe (Bruce Willis)	To learn how to use Cole's powers for good.	To reconcile with his wife Anna.
Cole Sear (Haley Joel Osment)	To learn how to use Cole's powers for good.	To tell his mother about his powers.

There is a triple climax in *The Sixth Sense* that brings these three goals to fruition through variations on family communication:

1. Cole learns to help the ghost of the little girl by delivering the video tape, incriminating the mother in the death of her daughter.

2. Cole tells his mother about his gift and delivers the message from Grandma.

3. Malcolm realizes he's dead and is finally able to whisper to Anna while she sleeps, telling her he loves her.

More common themes with sample films...

Family Ties: *The Fighter, War of the Worlds, The Blind Side, Winter's Bone, The Godfather*

Faith, Hope: *Signs, The Book of Eli, The Lord of the Rings: The Two Towers, The Shawshank Redemption, Contact*

Time: *Cast Away, The Curious Case of Benjamin Button*

Second Chances: *Million Dollar Baby, Seabiscuit, Hoosiers*

Social Status: *Titanic, Eyes Wide Shut, Match Point*

Friendship: *The Bucket List, Mean Girls, Thelma & Louise, Stand By Me*

Dealing with loss: *Minority Report, The Rabbit Hole, Inception*

Identity: *Milk, The Bourne Trilogy, Memento, Little Miss Sunshine, A History of Violence, Blade Runner*

The Nature of Love: *Shakespeare in Love, Emma, How To Lose a Guy in 10 Days*

Sin and punishment: *No Country For Old Men, Unforgiven, Sling Blade, Crimes and Misdemeanors, The Girl with the Dragon Tattoo*

The Underdog becomes a hero: *Transformers, Paul Blart: Mall Cop, Ratatouille, Rocky, The Verdict*

The Cost of Genius: *Shine, Amadeus, Good Will Hunting*

Revenge: *The Punisher, Taken, Payback, Munich*

The oppressed rise up: *Avatar, The Matrix, Dances With Wolves, Braveheart*

"BIG" THEMES

I've noticed that the bigger the film, the more broad the theme tends to be.

For example, the theme of *I am Legend* is "Light up the darkness."

That's it. Light up the darkness.

The theme of *Shrek* is obvious: Embrace your inner ogre.

If you want to appeal to a billion people all over the world, you should probably keep it pretty simple and universal.

But you occasionally get a huge film that tackles a more complex idea.

Let's use *The Dark Knight*, written by Jonathan Nolan, Christopher Nolan and David S. Goyer, as a case study, and you can read the Full Story Map in the Appendix.

THE DARK KNIGHT

The Dark Knight is an expert example of building an active story around a powerful, controlling Theme.

In a movie, especially a superhero action thriller, there must be HIGH STAKES with SERIOUS CONSEQUENCES. Life or death. Loyalty or betrayal. Love or Duty.

In *The Dark Knight*, the screenwriters wisely push the story to the extremes of the conflict. To find those extremes, I'd surmise that they began with Bruce Wayne/Batman's character and mythology and used those elements to push him into an impossible situation.

Here are three "essential truths" of Bruce Wayne/Batman:

1. Bruce Wayne has sworn to protect the people of Gotham City.

2. Bruce's alter-ego Batman is the only thing that can protect them.

3. Bruce's one rule is not to kill.

The screenwriters will push Bruce into a position where he has only two options:

- Give up his identity as Batman and turn himself in to the authorities, or...

- Kill The Joker.

In other words: an impossible choice.

This is what great drama is built upon.

The glue that holds it together is the theme of The Dark Knight:

Desperation pushes men to act in self-destructive and chaotic ways.

The writers use theme to create Bruce's actions and the trials that he will face in his fight to achieve his goal. This is why I call it the "controlling" theme; it can be used to essentially dictate a character's actions and dialogue and guide the plot of the story. It maintains the crucial "story focus" needed to hold a Reader's attention.

When in doubt about where to take the plot and what to make your character do...look for the answer in your theme.

I imagine that the writers began by making a list of extreme actions (things that Bruce Wayne would normally never do) that would express this theme:

- Bruce puts faith in a politician: District Attorney Harvey Dent.

- Bruce ignores the advice of Jim Gordon, Alfred, Harvey Dent, Lucius Fox and Rachel and decides to give up his identity.

- Bruce tortures a suspect in an interrogation.

- Bruce steals Lucius' technology and uses it to infringe on the privacy of all of Gotham's citizens, whom he has sworn to protect with honor.

- Bruce lets Batman take the fall for murder.

It then becomes the screenwriters' job to force Bruce into a position where he would logically (within the heightened "world" of a Batman movie) perform these actions. Since a great script focuses on a protagonist that drives the story with their active decisions, it's not hard to think that the above list of actions formed the basic spine of the plot, the signpost story beats that make up the "Full Story Map."

This theme also forces other characters to take irrational action. For example:

- Harvey Dent tortures a paranoid schizophrenic for information.

- Jim Gordon fakes his own death, keeping the truth from his family.

And it "controls" the goal of the Antagonist, The Joker:

- The Joker hatches an intricate terrorist plot based on fear that pushes the mob, Batman and the civilians of Gotham City to the point of desperation.

Ultimately, the screenwriters used their unique theme to construct an active story with multiple lines of action and a large ensemble of characters that fills 2 hours and 24 minutes of screen time.

It also seems likely that it was a theme relevant to the times: the post-9/11 "War on Terror" era in America and abroad. The theme had *urgency*. And it took a well-known character that we've seen portrayed in several films into new dramatic territory.

In conclusion, if you know what your story is *about* – the idea you want to *explore* or *what you want to say* – then the blank page will not seem so daunting.

FROM THE TRENCHES:

SCOTT ROSENBERG TAKES IT TO THE EXTREME!

I went to an industry event with a new business card. On the back of the card I had printed the logline for my screenplay, a supernatural action thriller that I like to describe as "Frankenstein meets Predator" as it's about a troubled scientist who loses his wife to a mysterious Yeti-like creature. He believes her to be dead, but years later he tracks down the monster's lair and finds that she is not only alive, but she has become the mate of the creature. The original draft had a very extreme way of showing this at the end of Act Two turn – the scientist finds his wife and the creature having sex. But I cut this as I felt it was too off-putting and would alienate readers and present problems for ratings.

The actual beat was not evident in the logline when I showed it to Scott Rosenberg (*Armageddon, Beautiful Girls, High Fidelity, Gone in 60 Seconds*) – it only said that he found the wife alive. He took one look at it and said...

"What if the guy gets there and the monster is f**king his wife?"

He had looked at the logline and immediately extrapolated the dramatic elements to their logical extremes.

I knew that I couldn't hold back. I needed to go back to my original idea.

On that note, it's time to...

VIII. GET EXTREME!

I love it when I see a movie or read a script and the writer is willing to "go there," to take the story to the extremes of the dramatic conflict. Not afraid to shock, offend or make their audience uncomfortable, but to be true to the story and the dramatic elements that they have built.

In *The Hangover*, the guys tell Phil (Bradley Cooper) not to leave the baby in the car alone and he argues, "I cracked the window!" Awful...but hilarious.

In *Million Dollar Baby*, Maggie (Hilary Swank) is not just hurt but she is paralyzed from the neck down. Her condition worsens and she asks Frankie (Clint Eastwood) to euthanize her. There is no last-minute save; he must end her life to allow his arc to come to fruition.

In *Sideways*, Jack (Thomas Hayden Church) has already had one affair and got his nose broken in 3 places, but he still insists on sleeping with the waitress, leading him to get caught by her husband. It gets worse when Jack makes Miles (Paul Giamatti) go back to the house to retrieve his wallet, and Miles gets chased by the naked husband. This represents the ultimate test of Miles' loyalty to his friend.

I see scripts all the time where the writer is unwilling to go all the way — one of the big reasons for this is that they consider the protagonist to be themselves. They can't have their hero lie, cheat or steal because it's something that they wouldn't do in real life (or at least they like to think they wouldn't). They also refrain from having something terrible happen to their protagonist (rape, paralysis, castration, the list goes on, people) because it scares them to think of this happening to them. But this is a story and your protagonist is a dramatic construction, *not* you.

Besides, your life is boring. Trust me, it would <u>not</u> make a good movie. At the least, you'd need to make up a lot of stuff.

So be prepared to be true to your story...to "go there"...to take the story to the natural extremes of the conflict. Go for it.

Why? Because not only does Drama = Conflict, but Hollywood is filled with thousands of bored workers reading the same old plot turns and story mechanics -- pull the seat out from under them and they'll love you for it.

IX. BILLY WILDER'S TIPS FOR WRITERS[1]

When I first watched *Sunset Boulevard* (1950) at home on DVD, I immediately noticed that Billy Wilder had structured his film exactly to the Story Map paradigm (Full Story Map in the Appendix).

As you prepare to structure your own narrative, here's some still-relevant advice from the late, great master...

1. The audience is fickle.

2. Grab 'em by the throat and don't let go.

3. Develop a clean line of action for your leading character.

4. Know where you're going.

5. The more subtle and elegant you are in hiding your plot points, the better you are as a writer.

6. If you have a problem with the third act, the real problem is the first act.

7. A tip from Lubitsch: Let the audience add up two plus two. They'll love you for it.

8. In doing voice-overs, be careful not to describe what the audience already sees. Add to what they are seeing.

9. The event that occurs at the second-act curtain triggers the end of the movie.

10. The third act must build, build, build in tempo and action until the last event, and then –

11. – that's it. Don't hang around.

---

1. From *Conversations With Wilder* by Cameron Crowe copyright © 1999 Cameron Crowe.

X.   MORE ON THE BEAT SHEET WITH EXAMPLES

Let's review the Beat Sheet with some dramatic sample beats from well-known films. In each list, I try to cite examples from multiple genres and also define a "classic" example of the beat, which means it's the perfect embodiment of all of the special characteristics of that beat from a time-tested film.

1) OPENING (PAGE 1-3):

Sweet spot: page 1-2

The first page of your screenplay is the most crucial page and the first ten pages are the most crucial section. You must open your script with a clear, concise scene that is easy to read, uses plenty of white space on the page and sucks in the reader. Your opening scene/s should feature these key characteristics:

- It establishes the ORDER (the unique world of the story) and the TONE (the "feel" of the script and movie).

- It expresses the THEME.

- It usually introduces the CENTRAL DRAMATIC QUESTION, an over-riding mystery that will not be solved until the Midpoint, End of Act Two or the Ending of the script. (Note: The true CDQ can be intro'd as late as End of Act One, but no later than that.)

- It probably introduces the PROTAGONIST, our main character/hero.

Classic Example – *Citizen Kane*: Charles Foster Kane utters "Rosebud" as he dies, launching our Central Dramatic Question, "What is Rosebud?"

Action – *Gladiator*: The opening shot is the hand grazing the wheat field in heaven, expressing the theme of "the afterlife." This is followed by the battle in Germania, establishing our hero as a great fighter and one that believes, "What we do in this life echoes in eternity!"

Comedy – *City Slickers*: Mitch and his two best friends run with the bulls in Pamplona, Spain. Mitch gets gored in the ass, causing him to vow that he will never go on another crazy trip again.

Drama – *There Will Be Blood*: When Daniel Plainview's leg is shattered while mining for gold, he puts the gold nuggets in his shirt and pushes himself across the desert using only his good leg, all the way to the claimant's office to collect his money.

BAD EXAMPLE *Superman Returns*: The opening launches the initial Central Dramatic Question of the film: "Where did Superman go for four years?" Eventually, we are told that he went back to the location of his home planet of Krypton based on a shaky scientific lead that there may have been survivors. Huh? So what did he do there and why did it take him four years? This is never answered.

2) INCITING INCIDENT (PAGE 8-10):

Sweet spot: page 10

The Inciting Incident is the first disturbance to the order that was established in your Opening scene. Key characteristics:

- It jump-starts the story into motion.

- It brings about danger, CONFLICT and chaos.

- It introduces the MAIN DRAMATIC CONFLICT and maybe the ANTAGONIST.

Classic Example – *Kramer Vs. Kramer*: Ted comes home late from work and his wife Joanna walks out, leaving him and their young son.

Titanic: Jack wins the ticket on the ship.

The Matrix: Neo meets Trinity, who tells him about the Matrix.

Spiderman: Peter Parker is bit by the radioactive spider.

The Hangover: The guys drive to Vegas.

Saving Private Ryan: The ramp is dropped on the landing craft and Captain Miller's men are mowed down.

When Harry Met Sally: Harry and Sally disagree over Harry's theory that men and women can't be friends. She bets him they can and will.

Erin Brockovich: Erin storms into Ed's office, the lawyer who lost her personal injury lawsuit case in the opening, and demands a job.

3) STRONG MOVEMENT FORWARD (PAGE 17-20):

Sweet Spot: 18

The protagonist truly takes the "first step" on their "core journey," the External line of action, even if they don't know it yet. Key characteristics:

- May be a conscious action by protagonist or they may be forced down a path. If the Inciting Incident was a slap, this is a push.

- True MOVEMENT on the inevitable main line of action, maybe in the form of a revelation.

- Perhaps the introduction of the DYNAMIC CHARACTER or MENTOR who beckons our protagonist on this journey.

- Must be going <u>forward,</u> not backward, so not repetitive of anything previous.

Classic Example – *The Wizard Of Oz*: Dorothy gets swept up by the twister.

Up: Carl lets loose the balloons and launches his house into the sky.

Inception: Saito offers Cobb the job of penetrating his competitor's mind.

The Wrestler: Randy accepts the rematch with the Ayatollah and meets Cassidy, his love interest.

Frozen River: Ray (Melissa Leo) decides to make her first smuggling run to save her home.

Black Swan: Nina gets the lead role in *Swan Lake*.

Stand By Me: The kids take their first step onto the train tracks, their "road" to find the dead body.

Gladiator: Emperor Marcus Aurelius asks Maximus to succeed him as leader of Rome when he dies, and return it to a democratic republic.

FROM THE TRENCHES:

ELIJAH WOOD
(The Lord of the Rings, The Ice Storm, Sin City)

"I'm attracted to great characters in the context of a script that isn't as interesting, but I'm just as interested in being a part of an entire piece that is brilliant even if it's a small part to play in that entire piece. I'm always just looking for something that I've never done and feels unique and special. And it's also just *gut*, what you emotionally connect with, and that can be a variety of things."

4) END OF ACT ONE TURN & DECISION (PAGE 25-30):

Sweet Spot: Turn: 27 Decision: 29

A surprising EVENT causes great conflict and a TURN in direction of the story (usually, a turn on the External line of action). The protagonist makes an active DECISION (ideally, a <u>shown</u> decision) in the face of this conflict and enters a GATEWAY—the story is propelled into Act Two in a new, unforeseen direction. Key characteristics:

- The plot takes a dramatic TURN in direction, not just a bump in the road!

- Stakes are heightened and new, more serious consequences arise.

- The protagonist formulates their first major PLAN OF ACTION that they will follow for Act 2A.

- It may signal a LOCATION CHANGE, but it *must* signal NEW DRAMATIC TERRITORY.

- External and Internal Goals, the Central Dramatic Question and the Act Two-A Story Engine must be established by the end of Act One, ideally by page 30.

Remember: TURN <u>and</u> DECISION. There must be something to propel the protagonist and us in this new direction and into Act Two. The protagonist's decision does not need to be onscreen, it can be implied. (For example, in *City Slickers*, Mitch's friends are pushing him to go with them on the trip to New Mexico for the cattle run — before he can answer, we CUT TO an aerial shot over the New Mexico plains and we know Mitch made the decision to go on the trip. New location and new dramatic territory, exactly 30 minutes in.)

Remember: 31-33 pages for Act One is acceptable, but a perfect 30-page Act One is <u>golden</u>. Readers will love you.

Classic Example – *The Matrix*: Neo meets Morpheus and is offered the blue pill or the red pill. Neo chooses the red pill and enters the "real world," a post-apocalyptic Earth run by machines.

The Hangover – The guys discover that the groom is missing and decide to follow their existing clues to find him.

The Social Network: Mark Zuckerberg is approached by the Winklevoss twins to build a dating website, but he blows them off and decides to make his own website, asking his friend Eduardo for startup money.

The Dark Knight: Batman meets with Harvey Dent and James Gordon about how to take down Maroni's crew. Batman vows to extricate Lao out of Hong Kong to bring him back to testify in court against Maroni.

The Wrestler: Randy the Ram is thrown into a ring with barbed wire, broken glass and an opponent with a staple gun. He decides to keep wrestling even though he's hurt, leading to a heart attack.

As Good As It Gets: Melvin is left with his neighbor's dog. He decides to take good care of it, showing his first affection for another living creature.

Rushmore: Ms. Cross brings a date to Max's play. Max throws a fit and announces he's in love with Ms. Cross.

Titanic: Rose and Jack share a stolen kiss.

Gladiator: Commodus, son of Marcus Aurelius, murders his father and marks Maximus for death.

Saving Private Ryan: Captain Miller is given the mission to go behind enemy lines to bring back Private Ryan. He accepts.

The Wizard Of Oz: Dorothy follows the yellow brick road.

Make sure to avoid:

- Repetition – Your turn and decision should be <u>new</u>, not just an extension of a previous beat. This is not just a complication, but a new direction.

- Going Back – Don't return to a previous location or previous dramatic territory. Keep pushing ahead—unless there is great <u>change</u> in the old location/situation.

5) FIRST TRIAL/FIRST CASUALTY (PAGE 38- 40):

The first major obstacle on the protagonist's new journey and the consequences that follow. The protagonist fails and pays a price. Key characteristics:

- A skirmish, foreshadowing a larger battle.

- A confrontation that raises the stakes, makes the threat "real" for the protagonist.

- The protagonist's failure leaves a consequence ("casualty").

- The casualty may be the death of an ally or a figurative death (e.g., the loss of innocence, a blow to the ego, a shocking revelation).

- Reinforces that the hero is now on an inevitable path, with no turning back.

Classic Example – *Saving Private Ryan*: The first firefight on their new mission; one of the platoon is killed.

Gladiator: Maximus races home to find his family murdered.

The Dark Knight: Batman brings back Lao, leading to the conviction of Maroni's crew, but the Joker unveils his first murder victim.

Meet The Parents: Jack gives Greg a lie-detector test, which Greg fails.

Sideways: Miles gets drunk on the double date, embarrassing himself.

> **5A) COMBAT (Page 45):** The First Casualty generates a more direct confrontation here. If the Trial was a skirmish, this is a BATTLE, more personal and with higher stakes.
>
> *Sideways*: Miles drunk-dials his ex-wife, confronting her about her new husband. She rebukes him.

The Matrix: Neo begins his combat training, spars with Morpheus.

Rain Man: Raymond has a panic attack in the airport, refusing to get on a plane. Charlie is forced to drive him cross-country in their father's roadster.

Rocky: Rocky brings Adrian back to his apartment. She initially resists, but he seduces her.

6) MIDPOINT (PAGE 50-55):

Sweet Spot: page 55

A DISASTER occurs DEAD CENTER in your story and RAISES THE STAKES, threatens the goal, and PUSHES THE ACTION TO THE CLIMAX with a new Story Engine(s). Key characteristics:

- False goals become true goals.

- Foreshadows and directly connects to the climax.

- Generates a new line of action or two that will culminate at the end of Act Two-B or the climax.

- Establishes a ticking CLOCK—a time deadline that escalates conflict and increases tension.

- The beat itself may be an emotional high point for your protagonist, but it must hold dire consequences and create a line of action/s that will push them toward the inevitable climactic confrontation. (An example of this would be a first kiss between two lovers who are committed to others, as in *The Notebook* or *Match Point*).

Classic Example: *Back To The Future*: Marty McFly must get his parents back together at the "Enchantment Under the Sea" dance or he will die. He must also use the lightning bolt that will hit the clock tower to get back to the future. Both of these goals will climax on Saturday night (the ticking "clock").

Titanic: the ship strikes the iceberg.

The Hangover: After a naked Asian guy pops out of the trunk and beats them all up with a crowbar, Alan admits that he put roofies in their drinks.

Up: Carl enters the dark dirigible of Charles Muntz, Carl's childhood hero and soon-to-be villain.

The Wrestler: Randy is rejected by his daughter.

The Wizard Of Oz: The Wizard orders Dorothy and company to bring back the broomstick of the Wicked Witch of the East.

The Sixth Sense: Cole's true power to see the dead is revealed. Also, Cole's mother rebukes him for moving Grandma's "bumblebee pendant," which foreshadows his Internal climax.

City Slickers: Mitch is forced by CURLY to deliver Norman the calf—this launches his love interest and foreshadows the External climax when he saves Norman from the raging river.

Sunset Boulevard: Joe succumbs to Norma Desmond's manipulations and becomes her lover.

Kramer Vs. Kramer: Just as Ted is bonding with his son and making single fatherhood work, he gets fired from his job, threatening his custody.

Rocky: Rocky Balboa reluctantly agrees to fight Apollo Creed. He is made fun of by Creed in the press conference and admits to Adrian that this upset him.

Inception: The team chooses an international flight for the mission.

The Social Network: Mark expands the site to Yale, Columbia and Stanford to attract Silicon Valley investors and he's rebuked by his ex-girlfriend.

Raiders of the Lost Ark: Indy finds the location of the ark in the map room and refuses to rescue Marion from the Nazis until he can save the ark.

6A) ONE HOUR WAR/TRIUMPH (page 60) (Optional):

Sweet Spot: page 60

The one hour mark in a movie, or page 60 in a screenplay, often brings a dramatic moment that may mark a direct confrontation, the introduction of a major character or a revelation. It's not required if your Midpoint occurs in the 50-55 range. But if you use it, it must be BIG in terms of heavy ramifications on the Protagonist's pursuit of their goals.

The Social Network: Sean Parker from Napster discovers "The Facebook" on a girl's computer.

Inception: Ariadne meets Mal in Cobb's subconscious, leading to a frightening confrontation.

The Wrestler: Randy kisses Cassidy (sets up his final decision to choose wrestling over love).

Raiders of the Lost Ark: Indy and Sallah open up the Well of Souls, finding the ark, but it is protected by hundreds of poisonous snakes.

7) DECLARATION OF WAR/ASSUMPTION OF POWER (PAGE 75):

Sweet Spot: page 75

The protagonist experiences a surge of strength, realizes their TRUE POWER and either initiates a direct attack on the Antagonist or prepares/TRAINS for the inevitable battle. Key characteristics:

- Moment of personal power

- Protagonist "fights back" after the devastation of the Midpoint.

- Protagonist throws down the gauntlet, issuing a challenge to himself/herself or the enemy.

- Protagonist is able to do something or see something that they previously failed at or did not understand.

Classic Example –*The Karate Kid*: Mr. Miyagi shows Daniel Laruso how he was actually learning to punch and kick when he was painting the fence and sanding the floor. Daniel realizes his potential for power.

Classic Example – *Rocky*: Rocky punches the meat, showing true confidence and strength for the first time.

Spiderman: Spiderman's first direct battle with the Green Goblin.

Up: Carl throws his old possessions out of the house, declaring war on Muntz to rescue Russell.

As Good As It Gets: Melvin agrees to drive Simon and Carol to visit Simon's parents. He opens up for the first time about his childhood, attempting to make a personal connection.

Sideways: Miles pulls out of his funk, showers and gets dressed up and goes to the restaurant where Maya works, determined to impress her.

Meet The Parents: Greg triumphantly returns Jack's cat Jinxy, winning over the entire family.

The Hangover: The guys work the blackjack tables with Alan's amazing "Rainman" skills, winning the money to pay the gangster to get the groom.

Rainman: Charlie Babbitt realizes that he was the reason Raymond was put in an institution, so he decides to take responsibility for Raymond as his brother.

Frozen River: Ray pulls a gun on the Russian smuggler, demanding her payment in full and standing up for two helpless Chinese immigrants.

The Wrestler: Randy asks his daughter to have dinner; she accepts.

8) END OF ACT TWO TURN & DECISION (PAGE 85-90):

Sweet Spot – Turn: 87 Decision: 89

Another major, shocking EVENT turns the story in a <u>new direction</u>, more dangerous than ever, forcing the protagonist to risk everything on a new course of action. Key characteristics:

- A shocking REVERSAL occurs, altering our original perception of an event, theme or character.

- The story "opens up" into NEW DRAMATIC TERRITORY and perhaps a new LOCATION as the threat worsens and maybe takes a new form.

- The hero HITS BOTTOM, feeling the dire CONSEQUENCES of their decision at the end of Act One.

- Plotlines CONVERGE to focus the story and to establish the final STORY ENGINE to push to the Climax.

- The protagonist is forced to make a NEW DECISION to "risk all" to achieve his/her goal, propelling us into Act Three.

Again: TURN <u>and</u> DECISION.

Classic Example – *Aliens*: When Newt is captured by the aliens, Ripley decides to risk her life to go back to find her.

Saving Private Ryan: They find Private Ryan, but he refuses to leave his platoon. Captain Miller decides to remain and fight, devising a plan to defeat the enemy tanks.

Titanic: Rose's family procures a lifeboat but she decides to risk her life to go back and find Jack.

The Silence of the Lambs: Hannibal tricks Clarice into revealing her childhood story of trying to save the lamb from slaughter. She is left totally alone and must fight on.

Being John Malkovich: Craig decides to remain inside John Malkovich, making him into a human puppet. He tells Malkovich's agent that he is leaving acting to become a puppeteer.

City Slickers: The group is left in the desert with no guides and 200 head of cattle. Mitch and friends decide to risk all and bring in the cattle themselves.

The Sixth Sense: Cole is given the videotape by the dead girl at the wake. He gives it to the father—the video incriminates the mother.

Rocky: After Adrian moves in with him, Rocky trains hard for the fight in the famous training montage.

The Hangover: The guys find the groom on the roof of the hotel and decide they can still make the wedding if they drive like maniacs.

The Wrestler: When his daughter rejects him for good, Randy quits his job and decides to come out of retirement to wrestle the Ayatollah.

The Incredibles: The family comes together and fights, in costume, for the first time as a team.

I Love You, Man: Peter (Paul Rudd) is dumped by his fiancé and he "breaks up" with Sidney (Jason Segel).

North By Northwest: Cary Grant dodges the plane in this famous sequence. The plane crashes, he steals a car and heads back to confront the enemy.

9) TRUE POINT OF NO RETURN (PAGE 100):

Sweet Spot: 100

An intense, high-conflict moment that conclusively sets up the final battle. A discovery or revelation that marks that from this point on, there truly is NO RETURN! Key characteristics:

- Ratchets the stakes and tension up to its ultimate peak as the threat takes on even more power.

- Just when you thought it couldn't get any worse...it gets worse!

- The protagonist makes their final <u>statement of intentions</u>.

- The protagonist formulates the <u>method of defeat</u>, finding the Antagonist's Achilles Heel, which they will exploit to defeat them.

Classic Example – *Rocky*: Rocky decides that his goal will not be to knock out the champion, but to last the full 15 rounds with him, which no fighter has ever done.

Die Hard: John McClane's wife Holly is taken hostage and John sees the duct tape, formulating his plan.

Juno: Juno's water breaks. She's having the baby.

Zodiac: Greysmith (Jake Gyllenhaal) is asked by his wife why is he throwing away his life to pursue the killer. He says he just has to look at him and make the man know that he knows his secret.

The Wrestler: Randy chooses wrestling over Cassidy. He grabs the microphone and tells his fans that they are his true family.

The Silence of the Lambs: Hannibal escapes prison and Clarice visits the home of the first murdered girl, finding clues that break the case and will lead her to the lair of serial killer Buffalo Bill.

Aliens: Ripley burns the nest of the alien queen, saving Newt and running back to the escape ship.

As Good As It Gets: Melvin invites Simon to stay with him and asks his advice in regards to Carol.

10) CLIMAX (PAGE 105-110):

Sweet Spot: 106

The FINAL DIRECT CONFRONTATION between protagonist and antagonist. Key characteristics:

- Brings together all lines of action.

- Is surprising, yet feels INEVITABLE.

- Answers the CENTRAL DRAMATIC QUESTION.

- The protagonist ACTS ALONE (or, at the least, they are the primary force in a team) to achieve their goal.

- Represents the <u>ultimate expression of the theme</u>.

- Results in a NEW RESTORATION OF ORDER.

Titanic: Jack dies; Rose blows the whistle and is rescued.

Gladiator: Maximus kills Commodus in the gladiator ring and dies.

The Sixth Sense: Cole tells his mother about his gift. Malcolm realizes he's dead and resolves with his wife.

City Slickers: Mitch ropes Norman the calf in the raging river and shows his wife and kids his new smile.

Kramer Vs. Kramer: In court, Ted forgives Joanna; Joanna wins the case, but decides to give Ted custody of their son.

Aliens: Ripley vs. the Alien Queen, womano a womano!

Make sure to Avoid:

- Other characters saving the day for the hero.

- "Deus Ex Machina" – an unmotivated force or illogical event appears and saves the day, conveniently removing the threat for the protagonist.

11) EPILOGUE (PAGE 110) (Optional):

Sweet Spot: As soon after the climax as possible.

A final scene wraps up the story, showing us the NEW ORDER (without *explaining* it) and leaving us with the proper tone as we exit the theater. Key characteristics:

- Shows the RESOLUTION to the main dramatic conflict, the answer to the CENTRAL DRAMATIC QUESTION and the FRUITION of the protagonist's Arc.

- BOOKENDS the story as a payoff from the Opening.

Titanic: The elderly Rose reveals to us she still has the diamond necklace. She casts it into the ocean.

Saving Private Ryan: The old man in the cemetery is revealed to be Private James Ryan. He honors the sacrifice of Captain Miller and his platoon.

Gladiator: The hand in the wheat field is revealed as Maximus' as he ascends to heaven to join his family.

The Hangover: The photo montage of the bachelor party that we never saw.

The Matrix: Neo issues a warning to the evil A.I. and flies off.

Star Wars: The medal ceremony. (Hey, where's Chewbacca's medal?!)

And that's it. Pretty cool, huh? Hopefully, the reminder of these scenes will inspire you to watch and story map these great movies.

But before you do, I suggest you write out a Story Map of your own, for a new script or an existing one, using the worksheet below. Don't worry about getting it *right* on this first pass, just write it.

THE WORKSHEET

Fill in the following STORY MAP WORKSHEET with your main dramatic elements (The "Basic Story Map") and your plot structure (The "Full Story Map") and try to make sure each element contains the characteristics as described in the above pages.

BASIC STORY MAP:

The Protagonist:

       Skill (their greatest talent/power):

       Flaw (their greatest weakness – the "Achilles Heel"):

       Misbehavior (a trait that consistently generates conflict; this may be the same as the Flaw):

External (plot, action) Goal:

Internal (character, emotional) Goal:

The Main Dramatic Conflict:

The Theme:

The Central Dramatic Question:

The Ending:

The Arc of Change:

LOGLINE:

FULL STORY MAP:

STORY ENGINES: <u>one sentence</u> (just one!) to describe the protagonist's major goal/need or the major plot movement of each of the four "Acts." (e.g., *Neo enters The Matrix for the first time and must use his newfound powers to battle an Agent.*)

ACT ONE:

ACT TWO-A:

ACT TWO-B:

ACT THREE:

BEAT SHEET:

ACT ONE:

1) **OPENING** (Page 1-3):

2) **INCITING INCIDENT** (Page 5-10):

3) **STRONG MOVEMENT FORWARD** (Page 17-20):

4) **END OF ACT ONE EVENT/TURN** (Page 25-30):

DECISION:

ACT TWO-A:

5) **FIRST TRIAL/FIRST CASUALTY** (Page 38-40):

      5A) **COMBAT** (Page 45):

6) **MIDPOINT** (Page 50-55):

      6A) **WAR/TRIUMPH** (OPTIONAL) (Page 60):

ACT TWO-B:

7) **DECLARATION OF WAR/ASSUMPTION OF POWER** (Page 75):

8) **END OF ACT TWO EVENT/TURN** (Page 85-90):

DECISION:

ACT THREE:

9) **TRUE POINT OF NO RETURN** (Page 100):

10) **CLIMAX** (Page 105-110):

11) **EPILOGUE** (OPTIONAL):

NOTES:

XI.   THE TEMPLATE FILM

I believe that that the practice of <u>written analysis</u> of films and screenplays (as opposed to just watching and reading) is the best way to learn about screenwriting.

To help develop your structure skills and your understanding of the Story Map, I suggest you write maps for your favorite films. This can also help you with a specific script. I am a big proponent of basing the structure of your screenplay on an existing movie that shares key attributes with your story. This is a great idea for any script, but it's especially helpful in the early stages of your writing.

Choose a template film available on video (and, ideally, one with a script available for download, although the script is not as important as the movie at this stage) that shares genre, themes, and elements of plot and character with your original screenplay. It doesn't have to match up perfectly; the connection is your choice.

For example, if you're writing a story about a family of superheroes, you should map *The Incredibles* to see how Brad Bird separated his Acts, where he placed his signpost beats and how they advanced the story through active means while developing his main characters and unique villain.

If you're writing a sports film, you might want to look at my map of *Rocky* and then map a more recent film, such as *Warrior* or *Invincible*.

I had a student who chose *21 Grams* as her template film and ended up adopting a similar non-linear scene structure—it turned out to be the perfect way to tell her story.

This exercise will force you to think about how the writer approached the story and solved problems, and you can compare it to your own unique Story Map.

THE MECHANICS

XII. THE SCENE LIST

Now that you have established the major "signpost" moments of your story and before we move on to the actual physical writing of properly-formatted screenplay pages, let's talk about the structure of your individual scenes.

With the Full Story Map complete, we continue to progressively add more detail to flesh out the story.

The next step is to build your complete Scene List, using your Full Story Map Beat Sheet as a template. The full scene list should be in the range of 40-60 scenes, depending on the complexity of your story. A transition, like a character driving from one location to another, is not a scene, unless it has a beat that advances the story. Which brings us to one of our most crucial Golden Rules...

If a scene does not...

a) Advance the story

b) Reveal crucial character

  or...

c) Explore the Theme

...CUT IT!!

The first directive is the most crucial: a scene must <u>advance the story by bringing about some sort of change</u>. If it does not, it can go.

As they say, a writer must be able to "drown their puppies." You must be ruthless in cutting scenes, even if it's one of your little darlings that contains your favorite line of dialogue in the whole script. If it's not <u>crucial</u>, you gotta cut it!

With that said, it can often give your story some extra style by having one "fun" scene that does not necessarily have to be there but yet exemplifies the spirit of your movie.

These quirky scenes are often the thing that the reader remembers the most in a script. Some inspired examples:

- *Fargo*: Marge has lunch with her Asian-American classmate.

- *Goodfellas*: The "What's so funny about me?" scene.

- *Boogie Nights*: The music studio scenes. Dirk and Reed record classic songs like *Feel, Feel, Feel My Heat!*

- *Anchorman:* Paul Rudd tries out his most exotic cologne, "Sex Panther," on the ladies in the news room, to disastrous effect.

One could argue that even these scenes advance the story in some way, but I'm guessing that if they were taken out we wouldn't necessarily feel a gap in the story.

I suggest you keep it to one "floater" scene that doesn't really advance the story, unless it's a comedy, in which case more might be welcome, but they'd better be heee-larious or they'll just sit there like fresh roadkill.

FROM THE TRENCHES:

DAVID & JANET PEOPLES
(*Twelve Monkeys, Unforgiven, The Prisoner*)

I had the pleasure of visiting David and Janet Peoples, a successful married writing team, in their home in the hills. They told me how their three-story house helped their writing method: his office was on the lower floor, hers on the top with the ground floor as "a buffer in-between." This gave them just the right amount of physical distance so they could maintain their own mental focus and make their individual contributions to their collaborations.

ACTIVE STORYTELLING

"Active Storytelling" is my term to describe screenwriting that consistently advances the story, brings about change, escalates conflict, raises the stakes, shows character through action, *shows* rather than *tells* and has an overall cinematic sense to it (it "feels like a movie"). It's no easy task, but you'll learn how to achieve it if you work hard enough.

Active Storytelling should be first practiced in your scene list. Check for scenes that are merely introductions, transitions, repetitions, "talking heads," or "reports" to characters of information that WE already know.

Here's an example of an inactive, repetitive scene list for Act One...

1. OPENING: JOE, 40s, is fired from his accounting job.

2. Joe drinks alone at a bar. He tells the bartender he just lost his job.

3. Joe has dinner with his wife SALLY and his two KIDS. He tells them he lost his job. His wife tells him he's sleeping on the couch until he finds a new job.

4. At school the next day, his son tells his teacher that his dad lost his job.

5. Joe drives to the unemployment office.

6. Sally talks on the phone with her best friend.

7. INCITING INCIDENT: At the unemployment office, Joe is told there's a job at the zoo.

8. Joe tells his DAD he lost his job.

9. Joe starts working at the zoo, cleaning the lion's habitat. As a prank, his co-workers shut the door and lock him in with the lions. The lion creeps toward him; at the last minute the co-workers open the door and Joe runs back inside, having peed his pants.

10. Joe sleeps on the couch.

11. STRONG MOVEMENT FORWARD: The next day, Joe is cleaning the lion habitat again. When he's done, he sees the lion is blocking the exit door. Joe puts his hand out and calms the lion. It nuzzles him. His co-workers can't believe their eyes.
12. Joe tells his family at dinner about taming the lion. Only his daughter believes him.
13. At school, his daughter tells her class that her daddy tamed a lion. They laugh.
14. Sally talks to her best friend, laughing about her husband, the delusional lion tamer.
15. Joe once again calms the lion and gets it to nuzzle against him.
16. TURN: Joe catches the eye of a TV PRODUCER, who offers Joe a job as the star of his own reality TV series, "The Lion Whisperer."
17. DECISION: Joe accepts the offer.

There's a good story in there but there's a lot of fat to trim, most notably, a lot of "telling" and not enough "showing." Notice the scenes with characters reporting information that WE already know, thus it's repetitive. Even if your characters don't know a certain thing yet, it's usually a waste of time to show them being told the information, so try to find a way to imply they know it or show them learning it in a way that does not rely on dialogue. Or, we may just assume they know it.

Here's an edited version with cuts in strikethrough and changes in bold:

1. OPENING: JOE is fired from his accounting job.
2. **Joe drinks alone at a bar. ~~He tells the bartender he just lost his job.~~ His credit card is declined, so he tells the bartender he's going to an ATM and will return soon, but he runs away. He's humiliated.**

3. Joe has dinner with his wife SALLY and his two KIDS. He tells them he lost his job. His wife **glares at him.** ~~tells him he's sleeping on the couch until he finds a new job.~~

4. Joe sleeps on the couch.

5. At school the next day, his son tells his ~~teacher~~ **grandpa (JOE'S DAD)** that his dad lost his job.

6. Joe drives to the unemployment office.

7. Sally ~~talks on the phone with~~ **meets her best friend at the mall. They run into a young, SINGLE GUY who shows interest in Sally.**

8. INCITING INCIDENT: At the unemployment office, Joe is told there's a job at the zoo.

9. ~~Joe tells his DAD he lost his job.~~

10. Joe starts working at the zoo, cleaning the lion's habitat. As a prank, his co-workers shut the door and lock him in with the lions. The lion creeps toward him; at the last minute the co-workers open the door and Joe runs back inside, having peed his pants.

11. Sally meets the Single Guy for coffee.

12. Joe's Dad stops by the house and sees Joe in his zoo uniform. He asks Joe's son if he likes that his daddy picks up animal crap for a living. The son laughs. Joe boils but says nothing.

13. STRONG MOVEMENT FORWARD: The next day, Joe is cleaning the lion habitat again. When he's done, he sees the lion is blocking the exit door. Joe puts his hand out and calms the lion. It nuzzles him. His co-workers can't believe their eyes.

14. Joe tells his family at dinner about taming the lion. Only his daughter believes him.

15. At school, his daughter tells her class that her daddy tamed a lion. They laugh.

16. Sally talks to her best friend, laughing about her husband the delusional lion tamer.

17. ~~Joe once again calms the lion and gets it to nuzzle against him.~~

18. TURN: Joe **rides the lion**, catching the eye of a TV PRODUCER, who offers Joe a job as the star of his own reality TV series, "The Lion Whisperer."

19. DECISION: Joe accepts the offer.

As you can see, I've cut static "talking heads" scenes and transitions, added beats that advance the story and fleshed out the story with a new character, Single Guy, while making other characters more active, like Joe's Dad.

The moment where Joe sleeps on the couch is a good example of not needing an "Intro" to a scene and showing over telling. In the first version, the wife tells him he's sleeping on the couch, but we don't see him sleeping on the couch for several more scenes. There's a delay and the payoff supports our expectation rather than subverting it, thus no element of surprise.

In the edited version, we see the wife glare at him and then immediately cut to Joe sleeping on the couch. It's perfectly clear that she kicked him out of bed as a revenge for his being fired and there's no need for an introductory explanation.

I see this basic construction a lot from newer writers:

A. A character tells other characters that he's going to do something.

B. The character does that thing, exactly as he explained he would.

C. The character reports back to the other characters that he did it and they discuss it.

Argh! Only scene B is actually advancing the story by showing us a beat of action. A and C are unnecessary and can be cut.

Making up a full scene list before you begin to write pages will prevent you from making these errors and wasting time writing a bunch of inactive scenes.

Some writers choose to write without an outline and just free-flow, but in case you can't tell, I'm anti-free-flow! I highly suggest that you don't do that because screenplays are all about STRUCTURE. If you write an undisciplined batch of scenes, you'll waste a LOT of time later cutting, trimming and rewriting to give it structure. (An exception to this might be if your inspiration for a story is a single, dynamic scene and you want to write out that scene first to "field-test" it before working up a Story Map.)

VISUAL ("SHOWN") DEVICES

Look for visual ways to move the story, communicate character or provide exposition.

One of my favorite shown devices comes shortly after the powerful D-Day invasion in *Saving Private Ryan*, which threw us into battle with no background on our platoon of soldiers. The battle is over, and we see Tom Sizemore kneel on the ground, pull an empty shoe polish can from his rucksack and fill it with dirt. He caps the can and we see it's labeled "France." Other cans in his bag are labeled "England" and "Africa."

In a very simple way, we learn that this is not an untested platoon – these men are war veterans. This is crucial because their Captain will soon sign them up for what could be a suicide mission. They are to risk their lives for a young soldier who has *not* proven himself in battle; Private Ryan is getting a free ride home because he lost his brothers in the war. This makes the men increasingly bitter as they continue on their mission, which develops the theme of sacrifice.

Let's say you need to tell us about your protagonist's childhood. A killer monologue could be great, but maybe you could substitute a few cans of shoe polish?

From the screenplay for *Juno* [written by Diablo Cody; Fox Searchlight pictures, Mandate Pictures], here's a nice visual device to show how Juno chooses Paulie as her boyfriend:

```
Bleeker walks down to the end of the
driveway and opens the latch on the mailbox.

At least one hundred containers of ORANGE
TIC TACS come pouring out in an colorful
deluge. They spill out onto the driveway.

Bleeker smiles.
```

It's almost always better to show, rather than tell. In *Armored*, we never fully invest in the protagonist because the elements that are intended to gain our sympathy, mainly that he's an Iraq war hero and his house is in foreclosure, are only communicated in dialogue. We don't feel the *urgency* when we don't see something for ourselves.

BALANCE

As you look at your scene list, you don't want 15 scenes in your Act One, four in your Act Two and 12 in your Act Three because this would be out of balance with the crucial structure of the Story Map. Remember the page counts for each of the four acts and try for your scene list to reflect these lengths in proportion:

Act One: 30 pages

Act Two-A: 25 pages

Act Two-B: 35 pages

Act Three: 20 pages

A good early goal is to have each of the four acts contain about the same number of scenes. You may find that your Act One has more than the others since there is more to establish. This is fine; just make sure it's not *too* out of balance.

It's also common to adjust the Full Story Map beats as you write your scene list. For example, to make your story move quicker, you may move your End of Act One Turn at page 28 up to the Strong Movement Forward slot at page 20, make your First Trial/First Casualty at page 40 into your new End of Act One turn at page 28 and move your page 45 "Combat" into the First Trial/First Casualty position at page 40. I often make the suggestion to "move up your beats" to my writers. But make sure that the new beats satisfy the proper characteristics as laid out in the Full Story Map chapter.

Trust me, if cutting and arranging beats makes your story move quicker, it's almost always a good thing.


```
There's nothing a reader likes more than a
tight script --
```

```
with a lot of white space
```

```
that's easy to breeze through!
```

FROM THE TRENCHES:

LESLIE DIXON
(Mrs. Doubtfire, The Thomas Crown Affair, Hairspray, Limitless)

I covered the novel "The Dark Fields" by Alan Glynn for Miramax Films, and they purchased the rights. The brilliant and glamorous Leslie Dixon was assigned to write the adaptation.

Later, she wrote me: **"I made Harvey (Weinstein) a proposition: I'd do the script for scale if I had NO MEETINGS AND NO EXECUTIVE INPUT."**

She also cannily put it in her contract that the rights would revert to her if they didn't make the film, which is exactly what happened and she took the project on her own as the writer/producer. She stuck with it through years of development and the movie opened at #1 as *Limitless* starring Bradley Cooper and Robert DeNiro.

The Lessons:

1. **Don't give up!**

2. **If you want creative control, get it in the contract!**

SCENE WORK

Firstly, follow the golden rule for scene length...

Start your scene as LATE as possible; end as SOON as possible.

This means cut to the MIDDLE of the scene. Open on the action already in progress. Hopefully it will be clear. Hopefully you won't need to EXPLAIN anything.

You don't need entrances and exits, most of the time.

You don't need to SET UP every scene, which I call...FORECASTING.

If we're going to see your protagonist at the grocery store in the next scene, she doesn't need to say "I'm going to the grocery store, to pick up some spinach and ricotta cheese for dinner tonight." Just CUT TO: THE GROCERY STORE! This of course relates to the all-important rule of...

SHOW, don't tell.

Now if we know the Bad Guy planted a bomb in the ricotta cheese section, then okay, maybe it's crucial that she tell US where she's going to escalate the tension! But what are the odds the Reader won't cringe when you pull out the tired ol' "explosive Ricotta" gag? Yeah, every brainless Hollywood blockbuster has worn that one out.

Ever heard of the ol' "If you didn't <u>see</u> them die, they ain't dead" rule? There's many examples of this rule, but one that comes to mind is *The Negotiator*: They never showed the guy that Sam Jackson gunned down, so when they reveal he's alive and Sam Jackson's not actually a killer, it's not a shock. I knew from the getgo that he didn't really shoot the guy. (*The Sixth Sense* is actually the flipside of this rule: we didn't see Bruce Willis die because we would have known he *is* dead.)

This is also an example of the next rule...

Be aware of the audience/Reader, especially what they know, and do not repeat this information.

Don't repeat info that WE (the Reader/audience) know. A good reader remembers every word.

Try to have a beginning, middle and end in your key scenes (use of "threes," like three acts), and end on a surprise.

This doesn't dictate length. Your complete scene with a beginning-middle-end could be one half of a page in length. And surprise us with a change at the end of your scene. It doesn't have to be a shocking reversal, just a change. Good scenes are about DISCOVERY; we discover something unexpected, something that subverts our expectations, not supports our expectations.

Think of the introduction of Jack Sparrow in the first *Pirates of the Caribbean* film: we see him proudly riding the mast, personifying a majestic captain of the high seas, until we discover that his shoddy boat is <u>sinking</u>. He steps onto the dock just as the ship disappears under the water.

Try for a <u>change</u> in each scene. Always try to <u>advance the story</u>.

This is where notecards and scene lists come in handy; you can review your scenes in outline form ahead of time and eliminate those that don't offer anything new or advance the story.

Try for Three-Scene Sequences (another use of threes).

This utilizes *cause-and-effect*. We are shown one thing that leads to another, that leads to another that offers the fruition of this movement. Three scenes which also form a beginning-middle-end. This also forces you to write logical follow-ups to your scenes to establish flow; *this happens* which forces our hero to make *this decision* which leads to *this confrontation*, which is resolved in *this way*. How you place those beats in your three scenes is up to you. E.g., you may have the hero making their decision at the end of the first scene, or maybe you should hold it until the second scene. Or best of all, a decision in each scene, to really show character through action. Up to you.

Unbreakable by M. Night Shyamalan is an example of some nice three-scene sequences...

1) David Dunn rides a train. When a pretty woman sits next to him, he takes off his wedding ring and tries to talk to her. She rebuffs him.

2) Dunn wakes up in a hospital, is told he was the only survivor of the train wreck and is unharmed.

3) Dunn's son and wife arrive to take him home. He doesn't touch his wife. They sleep in different beds.

4) Dunn gets a message on his windshield, asking him if he's ever been sick.

5) Dunn asks his estranged wife if she remembers him being sick; she doesn't know. Dunn leaves a message with his boss' secretary, asking if he's ever had a sick day.

6) Dunn's Boss gives him a raise, thinking this was his ploy to remind him that he never had a sick day.

7) Elijah tells Dunn, in front of Dunn's boy Joseph, that he believes he is a superhero.

8) Dunn thinks he's crazy and tells him about being injured in a car crash when Dunn was in college.

9) Dunn goes home, checks his pistol and looks at some news clippings; the train crash where he was unscathed is juxtaposed with the clipping from the car crash that injured his knee and ended his football career.

10) Dunn screens a Strange Man out of the line at the football stadium.

11) Dunn tells Elijah he saw the image of a "silver gun with a black grip." Elijah tells him he should develop this instinct, like a super-power. Dunn thinks he's crazy.

12) Elijah follows the Strange Man, sees that he has a silver gun with a black grip in his belt.

13) Dunn lifts 350 lbs. in front of his little boy Joseph. Joseph thinks he has super strength.

14) Joseph gets into a fight at school, trying to be a hero like his dad.

15) Joseph finds his dad's gun and aims it at him, thinking he'll be able to repel the bullet.

I'm leaving out many details for the sake of brevity, but this is the basic scene progression of the first half of the film and it's built on threes. Shyamalan expertly advances multiple lines of action in a single scene by compressing action into the same scene. For example, Elijah sees the gun in the Strange Man's belt because he's fallen down the stairs, which breaks his legs. This injury forces him to meet Audrey, Dunn's wife, who is a physical therapist who will be working with Elijah on his legs. Elijah's probing of information about Dunn's injury in the car crash will eventually lead us to find out the truth: Dunn faked the knee injury, for love, so he could be with Audrey. This pushes us closer to Dunn showing to us that he is, indeed, a superhero.

This type of organic, yet surprising progression of scenes utilizes possibly the most important technique of all:

Focus on SETUPS AND PAYOFFS.

One could say that a screenplay is merely Setups and Payoffs, nothing more; I wouldn't disagree. Often the strongest payoffs come in the third act and are set up in the first act. Remember how Chekhov said "If there's a gun on the mantle in Act One, it must be fired in Act Three!"

The best use of this technique recalls Billy Wilder's advice...

"Let the Audience put two and two together. They'll thank you for it."

A payoff is always best when WE get to recognize it, without it being explained to us. Like in the end of *The Blair Witch Project* when we see the kid facing the wall, we recall that quick story at the beginning of the film about the killer who made his victims face the wall. It's not explained to us, the image is enough. We remember and make the connection. Same goes for the climax of *The Silence of the Lambs* when Clarice enters the home of Jame Gumb and sees the moth land on the chair. We now know she realizes she's facing Buffalo Bill, the serial killer she's been tracking for the entire film. Her knowledge has caught up to ours.

At the Midpoint of *The Godfather*, when Michael Corleone finds the hidden gun in the bathroom of the Italian restaurant, we expect him to come out of the room blasting, just as his older brother Sonny told him to do (recall Sonny's infamous line: "I don't want my little brother coming out of that bathroom with just his dick in his hands."). But Michael doesn't do that. He sits down at the table with Capt. McCluskey, his target, and he waits. This increases tension and completely subverts our expectations for this payoff, so when he finally pulls the gun, it's happened in a way we didn't expect and it's a very satisfying release to the tension of the scene. That's good writing.

In Woody Allen's *Match Point*, the protagonist goes hunting with a shotgun with his father-in-law in the first half of the story, and in Act Three he uses that shotgun for other purposes. Shades of Chekhov?

ESTABLISH "THE RULES!"

It's incredibly important to establish the rules of your dramatic world as soon as possible so the reader does not get frustrated due to unanswered questions. Clarity is king.

This is especially true in genre stories — supernatural, science fiction, horror, etc. We must know what can and can't be done.

For example, in the film *Jumper* it's established that the protagonist can only teleport to places that he's seen, either in person or in a photograph.

In *Inception*, there's about 756 rules that are explained during the course of the movie. I counted.

In *Ghostbusters*, they can't cross the streams.

You get the idea.

Here are three examples of failure to establish rules:

Eagle Eye: Once we know the woman's voice is a computer, not a real person, all logic goes out the window. We don't buy it since we don't know the "rules" of it, and we have too many questions in our head. This kind of huge pull-the-rug-out reversal must be earned in active ways or it can backfire.

The Village: Same here — at the end of Act Two, we learn the monsters aren't real, just costumes that the elders wear to scare the youth into not leaving the village; but one minute later, our heroine is being stalked by one of these monsters in broad daylight! Is she in danger or not? We're confused as to how to feel.

The reveal is that the monster turns out to be the town dummy wearing one of the costumes, which makes sense after the fact, but it would have relieved a lot of confusion if we would have known this *before* his attack so the tension would have rightfully come from her being in peril, rather than confusion on our part.

The Time Traveler's Wife: In this film about time travel, they don't establish the rules of time travel! It's never fully clear what our time traveler can and can't do, and what seem to be rules are contradicted. While watching this film, I was constantly "in my head" asking questions about *how* and *why* things were happening. It made me want to travel back in time to prevent this movie from being made.

This same concept is also true when establishing <u>tone</u>. Martin Scorsese has said that one of the reasons he opened *Goodfellas* on the flash-forward to the scene where Joe Pesci stabs the guy in the trunk of their car (which was not how the original script began) was to establish that this was a brutally violent movie so the audience would be prepared for more violence to come.

A WRITING TIP

Here's a helpful rule that can really improve your output...

Always finish the scene you've begun.

Or another way to put it...

Always write at least one complete scene, every time you sit down to write.

This rule will force you to get in the habit of making real progress when you sit down to write, as opposed to just reading over your previous writing and making editorial changes. When writing your first draft, you must keep moving forward. With this standard, you will always be moving forward, even if it's just a 1/2 page scene. It may be a short scene, but at least it's a new scene! Cross off another bullet point on your scene list.

And when you're tired and cranky and don't feel like writing and it's not coming, then this rule will force you to wrap it up quickly, which is an exercise in keeping your scenes short and to the point!

It also comes in handy when you have a very energetic writing session and you write two or three scenes; then if you don't feel like writing the next day, you can skip that day because you're ahead of schedule! Or vice versa: if you miss a day then you should hold yourself to write at least two scenes today. If you use this "a scene a day" rule then you will find your screenplay taking shape rather quickly.

XIII. FORMAT – LITTLE TRICKS AND PET PEEVES

Writing in correct format is not as simple as buying a popular screenwriting software application. Your screenwriting program cannot format your script correctly if *you* don't understand how to use correct format.

For this chapter, I'll assume you know the basics of screenplay format; if not, then feel free to shoot me an email and I can send you a short primer, or you can check out one of the many books and articles out there on the subject. With that said, there are some key points and observations I'd like to make that I haven't seen mentioned in other sources.

The most important thing to remember with format is to BE CONSISTENT. If you cap LOUD NOISES, then you must cap every LOUD NOISE.

This means you must be <u>detail-oriented</u>.

Some of you just aren't detail-oriented enough to spot tiny changes in grammar and format so your writing turns out sloppy. While editing your script, you might not notice the difference between these two slug lines/scene headings...

```
INT. CONFERENCE ROOM - DAY

INT. CONFERENCE ROOM -- DAY
```

The first uses one dash and the second uses two dashes. This is important, because you can drive a reader crazy by constantly wavering between the two styles.

If your response is "Who cares?" then you're going to have a tough time with screenwriting. Capable screenwriters notice every little detail on the page...and so do <u>readers</u>. So be consistent, ferchrissakes. And next time you use that term, don't spell it "For Christ's Sakes;" spell it like you did the first time!

GRAMMATICAL KISSES OF DEATH

I'll say this only once.

If you can't differentiate between the following words then I will make it my mission in life to hunt you down and put a bullet through your laptop so you never inflict this ignorance upon me or anyone else in the world...

- Your and You're

- Lose and Loose

- Their and There and They're

- It's and its

I'm serious. Don't test me.

SLUG LINES/SCENE HEADINGS

```
INT. CONFERENCE ROOM -
DAY

INT. CONFERENCE ROOM --
DAY
```

In the above slug lines, which is correct, one or two dashes? The answer is both are correct, as long as you only use one type consistently throughout the script. That also goes for the period after the INT or EXT.

FROM THE TRENCHES:

TONY MOSHER, screenwriter, development professional (formerly of Schrader Productions, Shooting Gallery and Miramax Films)

"The more scripts you read, the quicker you're able to pick up on the warning signs that this script is going to suck. More often than not, you can tell by the end of the first page whether or not you're in good hands."

These are all correct, as long as you pick one and stick to this same construction for each slug line...

INT CONFERENCE ROOM - DAY

INT. CONFERENCE ROOM -- DAY

INT CONFERENCE ROOM -- DAY

INT. CONFERENCE ROOM - DAY

You can even get fancy and use a period instead of a dash, as long as you do it every time, but for the record, I don't advise this as it looks pretentious...

INT. CONFERENCE ROOM. DAY

Speaking of slug lines...to **bold** or not to bold?

INT. CONFERENCE ROOM - DAY

I used to hate to see bolded or underlined slug lines, until a friend told me he worked with Scott Frank (*Minority Report, Get Shorty*) and Scott Frank bolded *and* underlined his slug lines so now my friend bolds and underlines his own slug lines, too.

Hey, if Scott Frank does it, then it's good enough for me. But, if you're going to do it, do it every time.

INSIDE, OUTSIDE, LET'S CALL THE WHOLE THING OFF

One error that irks me is the addition of INSIDE after INT., which is repetitive. (You guys know that INT. means INTERIOR and EXT. means EXTERIOR, right?) For some reason, I see this error a lot.

For example...

INT. INSIDE OF LIVING ROOM - DAY

...should be...

```
INT. LIVING ROOM - DAY
```

...and...

```
EXT. OUTSIDE DRY GOODS STORE - NIGHT
```

...should be...

```
EXT. DRY GOODS STORE - NIGHT
```

USING A MASTER LOCATION

How you establish a master location, like a house, and then cut to a location within it, like the kitchen, is up to you. For example, you could use...

```
INT. MASON HOME - LIVING ROOM - DAY
```

or you could just use...

```
INT. LIVING ROOM - DAY
```

...and then when you cut to other rooms in the house you can do a full slug...

```
INT. KITCHEN - DAY
```

...or a "short slug" like...

```
INT. KITCHEN
```

...or just...

```
KITCHEN
```

...since we've already established the master location of the Mason home.

Pick your convention, make sure it's clear and stick to it — the Reader will catch on and won't even notice it after a while.

<u>UNDERLINING</u> AND *ITALICS*

Use underlining and italics in your description and dialogue very rarely. Only use them when something <u>must</u> be emphasized, and only *if* this will insure the reader's understanding of this moment.

I used to be anti-italics because they weren't classic formatting – scripts used to be written on manual typewriters, so the only way to emphasize a word was to put it in CAPS, <u>underline</u> it or to use

white space.

And those should still be your main methods of emphasis, in my humble opinion (with underlining being the most rarely used), but the occasional italicized word is fine. It's not 1932 anymore and everything we read nowadays uses italics – they're a part of our written vocabulary – so why not use them in your screenplay every now and then?

Speaking of which, another part of our modern writing is the use of only one space after a period and before the following sentence. The standard in screenplays used to be to double-space after a sentence.

Here's one line. Here's the next.

But it's okay now to only single space before that next line since we are so used to seeing that done on a daily basis in print (it also has something to do with uniform-sized characters and Truetype fonts on your computer, as a friend tried to explain to me before I fell asleep).

Here's another line. Here's the next.

Either way works fine for the reader. It's your call.

FLASHBACKS

Personally, for flashback scenes, I prefer to use this simple format...

INT. CONFERENCE ROOM - DAY (FLASHBACK)

...then the reader, like the audience, knows immediately that we're in a flashback.

If the audience is not meant to know it's a flashback at first, but eventually figure it out as the scene goes on (a pretty common technique these days, especially in indie films), then leave off the (FLASHBACK).

Other ways you can show a flashback might include a title to appear on the screen...

SUPER: <u>1942</u>

...or an aside to the reader in the description...

We're back in Mr. Stebbins' conference room but it's now 1942 and the room is filled with pipe smoke.

...or just put the year in the slug line...

INT. CONFERENCE ROOM - 1942 - DAY

Diablo Cody uses the (FLASHBACK) and also italicizes the slug line and description in *Juno* (also notice that for some reason she doesn't put the V.O. for Voiceover in parentheses. I'm not a fan of this technique, but she's consistent with it so it isn't an issue)...

She hangs up the phone.

                    JUNO V.O.
          I hate it when adults use the term
          "sexually active."

INT. HEALTH CLASS - DAY (FLASHBACK)

A HEALTH TEACHER in slo-mo puts a condom on
a banana.

                    JUNO V.O. (CONT'D)
          I guess Bleeker hadn't done it
          before, and that's why he got that
          look on his face.

USING CUT TO'S

You don't need to use CUT TO: after each scene, because the new slug line infers a change in scene, but some writers choose to use it. If you do, then (do I really need to say this again?) just make sure you ALWAYS use it.

                                        CUT TO:

Personally, I only use CUT TO: for a really dramatic transition, like a MATCH CUT, or if it will be difficult for the reader to understand the transition without it. I recommend against using it after every scene as it will add more length to your script. (Who wouldn't like an extra page of script?) Also, there will be fewer distractions to the progression of the reader's eye down the page.

"BEAT OUT" YOUR DESCRIPTION

You must keep your description paragraphs lean. Think of description in terms of *showing us the movie as it plays on the movie screen in our heads*, LIVE, in shots but without using camera references. Don't describe the shot as a visual—show us the action in a manner that captures the feeling of it.

Try to keep your description paragraphs two to four lines thick. Not two to four *sentences*, but two to four lines on the page, margin to margin. For example, this would be a two line block of description, even though it's one sentence:

Juno and Leah slurp giant slushies and sift through a pile of Penny Savers.

There should be plenty of white space on every page, with a nice balance of description and dialogue. Here's a sample of a page from *Black Swan*, written by Mark Heyman, Andres Heinz and John McLaughlin [Fox Searchlight Pictures, Phoenix Pictures]. Squint your eyes and look at the page as a whole, noticing the balance of black and white.

Now, compare the *Black Swan* page to this poorly balanced example, with way too much ink, from this obscure novelist named Stephen King. This is a page from his own script adaptation of his novel, *Desperation* [Touchstone Television] (please excuse the crooked scan):

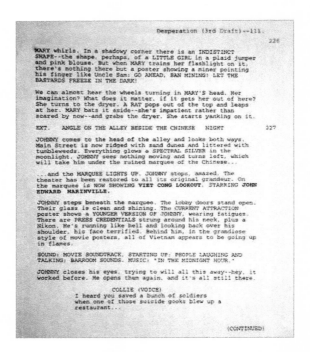

Now those are some Dark Towers of text! (I'll be here all week, folks.)

DON'T "DIRECT"

Repeat after me: I am the screenwriter, not the director.

Writing MEDIUM SHOT in your description means nothing. How can I picture the same exact medium shot as you? It's impossible to paint a picture with words such that the reader will see the exact same image as the writer. So don't bother, just tell the story. Actually, just <u>show</u> the story.

A few crucial directions are okay. For example, if your character is reading a letter and you need to show a close-up of the text on the letter, you could use a description like...

CLOSE ON LETTER: "I don't love you anymore."

The general rule is that you should only include a direction if the audience would not be able to follow the story without it. If you have a sniper in the wings of a political convention and you need to show his target, you may need to use something like...

POV RIFLE CROSSHAIRS: On President Dickinson!

The occasional ANGLE ON or PULL BACK is fine, but don't go nuts with a ZOOM IN HARD THROUGH TELE-PHOTO LENS! Spare us your directorial vision and technical prowess, please.

DON'T OVER-USE CAPS, PARENTHETICALS AND TRANSITIONS

Don't cap each character's name every time – some pro writers do this but I find it annoying to read, plus it can be confusing when trying to remember if this is the introduction of a new character or we've seen them before. I suggest you only cap a character's name in description upon their first appearance on screen; this is a MUST.

Don't include a parenthetical cue like (softly) above every dialogue block and don't drop a DISSOLVE TO: or FADE OUT: after every scene.

Don't use too many variations on DAY or NIGHT.

You will drive a reader batty with too many cues like this:

```
EXT. CONCERT HALL - MOMENTS LATER

EXT. CONCERT HALL - SAME TIME

EXT. CONCERT HALL - THREE MINUTES HENCE

EXT. CONCERT HALL - SEVERAL DAYS LATER

EXT. CONCERT HALL - AUGUST 1ST - TWILIGHT
```

The occasional NEXT DAY or DUSK or MAGIC HOUR or EARLY MORNING is fine, but don't get too fancy — stick to DAY and NIGHT 90% of the time.

USING CONTINUOUS

I see a lot of confusion with using CONTINUOUS. It is used only if a sequence changes to a new location with no break in the timeline. E.g.,

```
EXT. WAREHOUSE - DAY
```

The speeding Camaro hits the cement dock and takes air...

```
CRASHES into the wall!

INT. WAREHOUSE - CONTINUOUS
```

The Camaro crashes through the interior wall, landing on its wheels and SKIDDING to a stop, only inches from the Rabbi, who is bound to a chair.

Another common use of CONTINUOUS is when cross-cutting between two locations that need to occur at the same time, like if the first location is a room with hostages tied to a ticking time bomb and the second location is outside the building where the hero is looking for a way in to save them before the bomb goes off.

SCENE NUMBERS AND PAGE NUMBERS

Turn off Scene Numbers. Scene Numbers are for *shooting scripts*—you are writing a *spec*, or submission draft, that's meant for the reader, not the cast and crew.

Make sure your page numbers are in the upper right hand corner and are also in Courier 12 pt. like the rest of your script. There should also be a period immediately after the number, like this...

```
                                                    12.
```

Turn off the page counter that shows how many pages the current scene has been running for. E.g., don't include this at the top of the page...

```
CONTINUED (4):
```

You don't want to remind the reader that a scene has been going on for four pages—that's a cue to them that you may be overwriting. And it crowds the page.

CHARACTER NAMES

If you're consistent with your format and punctuation, soon the reader won't even notice it as their eye moves quicker down the page. The same goes for CHARACTER NAMES above dialogue; eventually, our eye skips over the name as we quickly recognize it in our peripheral vision. For this reason, you don't want to name two characters with the same first initial, e.g.,

```
                    DANA
          Hey Danny, how's it going?


                    DANNY
          Good, Dana, hey, guess what I
          learned today?
```

>   DANA
>   What?
>
>   DANNY
>   That our names are very similar
>   so in a two-person dialogue scene
>   like this one, the reader's eye
>   gets confused and mixes us up.
>
>   DANA
>   Son of a b-!
>
> -the reader's head EXPLODES!

You might have the urge to give a married couple or siblings the same first initial in their names, but I warn against this. It may seem cute to you that the triplets are named CATE, CAITLYN and CARY, but to a reader, they will wish for three anvils to be dropped on the three adorable mop-tops of those three obnoxious cherubs.

This recalls my **"You're not J.R.R. Tolkien" Rule**:

J.R.R. Tolkien can name two separate villains SARUMAN and SAURON, which is a <u>horrible idea</u>, because he's J.R.R. Tolkien. You can't because you're not.

An adjunct to this is my **"Mike Teavee is the worst character name ever" Rule**, which states as follows:

Roald Dahl can name a character who watches too much television, MIKE TEAVEE, which is pretty much the definition of <u>on the nose</u>, because he's Roald Dahl. You can't because you're not.

Whew. It feels good to get those off my chest.

A final, serious tip in regards to names: don't bore the reader with a cast of stiff "whitebread" names. If your characters all have names like JOHN SMITH, HERB DUNCAN, JILL JOHNSON, and DONNA WHITE, not only do their names not say anything about their character but they tend to run together and it's hard to remember them.

Which hitman are you going to remember? MICHAEL or BUTCHER BOY?

Which school teacher sticks out for you? MRS. JOHNSON or MRS. SCHAUDENFREUDE?

Now that we've got those basic tips out of the way, let's go deeper into communicating your story on the page.

XIV. TOOLS OF THE TRADE
(A.K.A. "You look dashing in your white space, MR. ELLIPSIS")

First, let's meet some friends.

There's the dash - the double dash -- the ellipsis...and the paragraph

break.

You can use these forms of punctuation to control pacing, tone, and to make a scene feel like a series of shots or beats as they would be shown in a movie. Here's an example of the double dash from the thriller *Eagle Eye* [Dreamworks SKG]:

```
RACHEL -- her heart skips a beat -- she
knows what's about to happen -- but she
can't do it, paralyzed--
```

Here's a section that uses dashes, underlining and "beat," which is the screenwriting term for *pause*:

```
INT PENTAGON - THE VAULT - CONTINUOUS

Callister leans somberly against the table.
Never thought it would come to this...

                    CALLISTER
          What I'm about to tell you can never
          leave this room.
               (beat)
          Three days ago we got what we
          Thought was iron-clad intel from the
          Brits.
               (beat)
          And we made the hit.

Latesha and Scott, completely shocked -
```

>   LATESHA
>   The White House said we weren't
>   responsible for -
>
>   CALLISTER
>   -- of course they did. We got the
>   wrong guy. And Aria knew it.

You'll notice the use of the dashes in the dialogue to show Callister is cutting off Latesha. This can be used in description or dialogue to show an abrupt transition — personally I prefer one dash rather than two dashes for a cut-off since it feels quick-

FASTER!

Here's an example from *Crash* by Paul Haggis & Bobby Moresco [Bob Yari Productions, Lions Gate Films] where one character cuts off another speaker in the middle of a question...

>   CAMERON
>   They were cops! They had guns!
>   Where do you think you're living,
>   with mommy and daddy in
>   Greenwich?
>
>   CHRISTINE
>   --Go to hell.

They inserted the double dash--with no space after it-- before the second line to really emphasize the rapid-fire response.

It's up to you how you're going to use punctuation on the page to make your reader FEEL the movie. Once you find your preferred style, stick with it and be consistent or you will drive the reader batty.

A note on the ellipsis: it can include spaces if you'd like, as long as you pick one style and stick to it. For example, you can use...no spaces. You can use... one space after the ellipsis. Or you can use ... two spaces, one before and one after (although I think this option takes up too much space and looks awkward). My least favorite option is a space in between every period . . . like that. I've seen it used, but I find it annoying, unless perhaps if it were used to capture the pace of a slow-motion scene.

But however you type your ellipsis, do NOT let your software *scrunch* it!

You know what I mean, when the three dots do…this? I…hate…this!!! They should…only…look like this...cool? The scrunched ellipsis is a sure-fire sign that you're not using a screenwriting package like Final Draft but rather a standard program like Microsoft Word, and that makes you look like an amateur. You can use Word or Celtx or whatever you want, as long as your format looks flawless and you turn off that evil scrunching option in the "Auto-Correct" menu.

SHOW, DON'T TELL

I can't teach you how to choose the best words to describe an action. Should Gerry *leap* or *alight*? Are Zoey's eyes *cold* or *hard*? Is the floor made of *flag stone* or *concrete*?

Is one *better* than the other? That's hard to say.

Does one evoke a tone or emotion that's closer to your intention for the scene? Yes. Remember, your goal is make the Reader feel the same emotion as they read the script as the Audience will feel when they watch the movie.

But not every Reader will agree. Different readers will read your script in different ways.

Ever had a friend tell you that a moment in your script is hilarious, when you meant for it to be sobering? Me, too. It sucks. (But hey, at least they're laughing, which means you got a strong emotion out of them.)

A key is to know when to break the rules. The biggest rule to follow is *Show, Don't Tell*, keeping in mind what the audience will see and hear in the scene. Consider the opening of the novel *The Big Sleep*, by Raymond Chandler...

> It was about eleven o'clock in the morning, mid October, with the sun not shining and a look of hard wet rain in the clearness of the foothills. I was wearing my powder-blue suit, with dark blue shirt, tie and display handkerchief, black brogues, black wool socks with dark blue clocks on them. I was neat, clean shaved and sober, and I didn't care who knew it. I was everything the well-dressed private detective ought to be. I was calling on four million dollars.

Fantastic voice. But here's what the audience sees in the movie...

EXT. MANSION - HOLLYWOOD HILLS - DAY

PHILIP MARLOWE, 32, dressed in a blue suit, strides up an elegant walkway toward a mansion with a view of overcast Los Angeles in the background.

Here's what the newbie screenwriter might write, "explaining" what we see with flat word choices and forms of "be" (is, are)...

DETECTIVE PHILIP MARLOWE, a private investigator in Los Angeles in the 1940's, is in front of a mansion, staring at it in an expensive blue suit and with a fedora. The sky is overcast and the ground is wet.

Here's what a more stylish screenwriter might write...

PHILIP MARLOWE, 32, strides up the elegant
flagstone walkway toward a magnificent home.
His blue wool suit costs much more than he
can afford but he knows it looks good and
looks can come in handy when your business
is trouble.

His eyes scan the manicured grounds, the
giant front door. He's confident...but
always cautious.

Here's another take, utilizing a bit more of "directing" but
not overly so, in my humble opinion, if we wanted to be
faithful to the source material...

PHILIP MARLOWE, 32, stares at the
overwrought mansion in front of him. His
blue suit is sharp and he knows it.

We see QUICK SHOTS of his outfit --

Silk display handkerchief, cutting at an
angle so precise it could set an instrument.

Black wingtips, polished to perfection.

The hat. Classic 1940s G-man fedora.

His eyes scan the front yard, confident yet
cautious, taking in the vintage Bentley, the
ceramic Sambo and the prize-winning azaleas.

He removes his hat and approaches the
monstrous front door.

Not bad, huh? But keep in mind you don't want to use this
much style in every scene, otherwise you'll pad the script
and risk missing your page targets for your signpost beats;
but it's pretty standard to do a bit of showing off in the
introduction of a key character, and this may come in handy

as "actor bait" to attract name talent that can't wait to live up to this sexy character snapshot.

You noticed I used the device of QUICK SHOTS, which is a shorthand that I find works well and tends to take up less space than A SERIES OF SHOTS, although the latter is effective for passages of time shown in a montage of shots...

A SERIES OF SHOTS

1) Nick walks onto the used car lot, is immediately approached by a laughing BALD SALESMAN.

2) Nick shakes hands with the Bald Salesman. He notices his hand is now sweaty.

3) Nick drives a shiny new KIA, papers in the window, down the road. A good-looking CHICK smiles at him. He gives himself a thumbs up.

4) Nick drives his Kia into his driveway -- the engine KICKS, smoke rises from the hood.

5) The Kia is up on blocks in the driveway -- Nick's shoes stick out from under it. His hand juts out, feeling for a wrench. His teenage SON, laughing his ass off, holds the wrench inches away from Nick's hand.

Poor Nick.

It helps to think of your description as beats of action within a scene, and pace out the shots as they would play on film, using white space, line breaks, and punctuation.

But you don't just want to list shots. You want to <u>say something</u>. You want to make your reader <u>feel</u> the way the audience should feel while watching this movie. It really irks me when I see a phrase that means nothing, it just sounds good —

> He lays his head down and sleeps the sleep of the dead.

But...the dead don't sleep. They're <u>dead</u>. And the above is a cliché that I've seen written too many times, in scripts and books.

Most importantly, it doesn't mean anything.

Another example, from William Goldman, no less, on page one of his screenplay *Absolute Power* [Columbia Pictures]...

> We'll find out more about him as time goes on, but this is all you really have to know: Luther Whitney is the hero of this piece.

His little "heads-up" to the reader is completely extraneous, considering that the scene is a well-written opening that SHOWS us Luther Whitney. He just wasted two lines on <u>page one</u>, the most crucial page in the entire screenplay, by telling us something that he had already shown us. If this were an unknown screenwriter, it would feel almost as if the writer wasn't trusting his own storytelling.

But he can get away with it because he's William Goldman. You're not, so don't do that. Here's another cliché...

> We'll call him JOE.

Who's we? Are *we* writing this story or are *you*, the writer? Normally, "we" is used to mean the audience, so is the audience collectively naming him Joe? Ugh.

This is not the most grievous crime, and a conversational style of description can work well, but the point is clear: curb your *telling*.

Here's an aside from *Juno* that feels much more organic and fun:

```
EXT. SUBURBAN STREETS - MORNING

It is now WINTER. The TRACK TEAM jogs in
formation, leaving tracks in the snow. Those
bastards never stop running.
```

BE BOLD, BEAUTIFUL AND BRIEF

Bottom line: your main job is to capture a moment in the most powerful way with the least amount of words possible.

Screenwriting is about brevity. Economy of speech.

Good screenwriting is <u>elegant</u>.

James Cameron described a shot of the sun glistening off the surface of the ocean as "Diamonds in oil." That's elegance.

Thinking of the big picture, you already know that one page of properly formatted screenplay equals one minute of movie screen time, and that I suggest you pace your script like modern movies are cut. But you still might have a question in the back of your mind...

What about all those deleted scenes on the DVDs?

Don't they want us to write more than they'll need so they have something to cut later in the editing room?

No.

You're a NEW writer. You need to show total command of your story and pace it like a modern movie. That's why you want to be <u>specific</u>. For example, you don't write...

```
Big action scene goes
here.
```

You need to craft every beat of that kick-ass action scene, using all the textual tools in your arsenal to create the tension and pacing that the audience will feel in the theater. Caps, white space, dashes, ellipses, underlining, line breaks, slug lines... the combinations of these devices are endless, just like the possibilities for a thrilling movie action scene.

FROM THE TRENCHES:

J. STEPHEN MAUNDER (*Tiger Claws I, II, III, The Veteran, Shadows in Paradise*)

"Anyone can punch and kick, but give one guy a banana and the other a coat hanger and you have an interesting fight. Put a spin on the mundane and it becomes memorable."

CHARACTER INTRODUCTIONS

How you introduce your characters is crucial. Again, you want to capture this unique person or creature in as few words as possible.

A common mistake is the contradictory character introduction...

```
BIGGS has the eyes of a
genius but the
personality of a dolt.
```

Seriously? While this may seem like an attractive challenge to an actor, it's just plain annoying to the reader. And I can't imagine an audience ever saying "Wow, that guy acts like an idiot but his eyes look so smart," can you?

CHERIE has the legs of a college cheerleader but coffee breath that would kill a charging rhino at twenty paces.

Okay, that's kinda funny if this were a comedy, but it's still a lot of *telling*. To *show* this, you would describe a sultry gal who slinks into a bar in a short skirt, approaches the first lucky gent she sees, says something to him, to which he promptly cringes, grabs his nose and runs away (or passes out, if this were a more silly movie...or turns and throws up all over the bar, if this were a Seltzer-Friedberg joint).

Another mistake is the intro with too much backstory that the audience couldn't possibly know...

JACE, 22, a machine shop foreman and part-time taxidermist who served two years in Iraq but was discharged for stealing potato skins from the mess hall, is the kind of guy who could kill and gut a pig but would never let a lady open her own car door.

I need a shower.

Or the pretentious/ "soul capturing" intro...

JANIE is a force of power in a wasteland of shattered dreams and small town dementia.

Uh...yeah.

Here's a nice capturing of a character without being ostentatious...

STEVE is the guy who was always too small to make the football team but still tried out four years in a row.

Here's some strong character introductions from produced scripts. From *The Beaver* by Kyle Killen...

WALTER, mid 40's, vacant, lies in bed fully dressed in a suit and tie.

From *Kick-Ass* by Jane Goldman and Matthew Vaughan...

A CAR pulls up and out climbs highschool senior DAVID LIZEWSKI. Not quite Napoleon Dynamite, but not quite Zac Efron either.

In William Monahan's Oscar-winning script for *The Departed* [Based on *Infernal Affairs*; Warner Bros. Pictures], he chooses to cap every character name in description, every time. In this excerpt, we've already met Colin and Barrigan but this is the first appearance of Mrs Kennefick.

COLIN and BARRIGAN (who Colin has moved to plain clothes) stand at the door, talking, or trying to talk, with a fearful MRS KENNEFICK. MRS KENNEFICK looks like she starts drinking whiskey at 9 in the morning.

From *Crash*...

FARHAD, Iranian, 50s, looks at the handgun and turns to his daughter DORRI, 25, who wears a blue suit and a bad mood.

That's a bit "on the nose" but it's in keeping with the style of the script.

It's best to also give your characters an action when we first see them.

Phil in *The Hangover* collects money from his junior high school students for their field trip and promptly pockets it for his weekend in Vegas.

Miles in *Sideways* moves his car, parked at an angle since he was drunk the night before, to let the gardeners park at his run-down apartment complex.

Max in *Rushmore* daydreams in class that he is celebrated by his teacher and peers in his prep school.

WRITING IN THE PRESENT TENSE A.K.A. *STAYING IN THE MOMENT*

The screenplay needs to read like a live transcript of what is playing NOW on the movie screen in our minds. The most simple way to think of it is that the script <u>shows</u> us what we SEE and HEAR.

Now.

Live.

How you show us what we see and hear is up to you, and what makes up your original voice.

Modifiers like *then, when, suddenly, eventually, usually, before* and *after* are not necessary and will often stick out to the reader. Technically, they're wrong as they contradict the live, "real time" tense of a script, but using a few can sometimes work better than not using them.

```
Joe skips down the sidewalk, a huge smile on
his kisser. He eventually reaches the end of
the sidewalk, steps off the curb and then,
suddenly...

He's hit by a LEXUS that comes out of
nowhere after slamming on its brakes, but
it's too late and Joe is sent flying 25
feet.
```

That's wordy, filled with adverbs and the second sentence is passive.

Here's what the audience sees and one way to write this scene in a more economical fashion...

```
Joe skips down the sidewalk, big smile on
his face. He steps off the curb and he's
```

```
SLAMMED by a Lexus!
```

There's several other variations you could use, like a double dash or an ellipsis after *he's* -- or beginning the second sentence with *Joe* or *A Lexus*. In the above example, the second sentence begins with a verb, SLAMMED rather than the subject (Joe or Lexus), but you'll notice that SLAMMED is in the past tense. It still reads okay, but SLAMS would be the technically *correct* option, so let's try that:

```
Joe skips down the sidewalk, big smile on
his face. He steps off the curb without
looking -- out of nowhere a LEXUS appears --
```

```
SLAMS into him!
```

Here, I had to mention the Lexus before the paragraph break into the second sentence to justify the SLAMS verb.

Getting hit by a car is usually going to necessitate a BIG verb. In other cases, you can go more subtle and still communicate the action. In fact, you can even skip over it and just imply the action. For example...

```
Ben doesn't notice Jim leave.
```

This reads better than:

```
Jim walks off. Ben is looking the other way.
```

It's not a huge difference, but I'd say the first one is more elegant.

The key is to use dynamic word choice, especially active verbs, along with a lean scene list, to achieve the critical "Active Storytelling."

It's also best to avoid too many present progressive tense verbs (the "gerund" forms, or "-ing" verbs). *Walks* is usually more effective than *is walking*. When you don't use the gerund verbs, it's also easier to avoid those lazy forms of "be:" the usage of *is, are, there is* and *there are*. You can always work a bit harder and...

USE STRONG VERBS!

Verb choice is a big part of writing effective description. Along with avoiding forms of "be" and the progressives, stay away from the dreaded "goes" and "comes."

Keep it second person present tense and use <u>strong, unique verbs that capture tone, emotion, and character.</u>

Unfortunately, I see a lot of this in description:

```
Jack goes to the sidewalk to his car, goes
inside the car.
```

```
Jack is inside the car, behind the wheel,
Shelly is coming out of the house.
```

Yuck.

Remember that this is happening NOW and it must be clear and interesting. "Nick is also in the room" is frustrating to the reader; where is he in the room? What does his body language tell us? What's he doing? What's the blocking of the actors in this room? I should be able to SEE it.

Your description shows us WHAT WE SEE and HOW TO FEEL — how do I know the tone of the scene by Jack "going" to the car or the refrigerator? But if Jack "charges" his BMW, or "shuffle-steps gracefully" along the catwalk...that gives some sense of emotion and style, right?

What if he "grits his teeth" the whole time, or he's "smiling a Cheshire cat grin" while performing these actions? These could be great ways to reveal character and tone.

Every word counts, even a little verb in one little description
sentence. So take some time to come up with that word,
make that verb unique, CRAFT every word in the sentence.

This all comes down to one of the most basic lessons in
screenwriting...

NEVER WASTE WORDS!! Which reminds me of a crucial edict.
Say it with me and speak it with relish, kind screenwriter...

Be elegant.

THE VOICE

XV. SUCK IN THE READER

If you practice your craft long enough, you're going to develop your "voice" on the page. This voice can (and probably should) change somewhat with each script you write, especially when switching genres, to capture the proper style and emotion for the reader, your substitute audience member. Let's explore this topic in more detail with more examples from produced screenplays.

Your voice comes out in Dialogue and Description, but I believe that dialogue is not quite as important as structure and description for spec screenplays submitted by a NEW writer. Dialogue may win Oscars for the big boys and get many an established pro hired on assignment, but for you, I say keep it as lean as possible. You still want to write distinctive dialogue for each character, but you must avoid the constant temptation to communicate exposition in dialogue.

You've probably heard about those industry types who read only the dialogue in a script. Well, that can happen, and it will happen if you bore the reader, so I'd contend that it's your job to make the reader WANT TO READ your description by seducing them with a compelling narrative voice that establishes TONE, PACING and EMOTION right off the bat, rather than just listing flat stage directions.

You need to suck in the reader.

This is not a license to pack each page with dense blocks of text and riddle them with landmines o' wit in the form of sarcastic asides, but rather a call to not waste a single word, while considering how the audience should feel at this moment in the movie.

It all comes down to word choice. This may seem obvious – isn't that what writing is, choosing the right words? But too many of you have been told to view your screenplays as "blueprints" for films, when I think you'd be better off approaching it as the "emotional cinematic template" for a film. It has to FEEL like a movie and it has to feel REAL. The only way to do that is to choose the perfect combination of words.

Description is more than mere blocking cues. It's true that the most important aspect of description is to show us what we see and hear, and it must be CLEAR above all else, but the reader does not want a shot list, they want two hands to reach out of the manuscript, grab them by their sallow cheeks and PULL THEM KICKING AND SCREAMING INTO THIS MOVIE.

We're all writing spec screenplays for a professional Story Analyst who reads flat, uninspired prose all the time. They're waiting for something fresh, something with LIFE. They're dying to read work by a writer who can really <u>write</u>, not just string together sequences. As I mentioned earlier, when I was on the job, I always reminded myself that I was looking for reasons to say "yes" rather than reasons to say "no." There's a big difference there; it's rooting for the writer to be good (so you can help some quality writing go up the ladder) rather than hoping they're bad (so you can just get through the script and be done with it). I believe that readers today are looking for the same thing.

You need to establish right off the bat that you are confidently taking the reader to a specific world which only *you* know in this way, at this time, in this manner, with this feeling. And the best way to do that is with a unique voice on the page, in description *and* dialogue, but first we're going to focus on description.

FROM THE TRENCHES:
LOUIS C.K.
(Louie, Late Night with Conan O'Brien, Saturday Night Live)

"I've hired a lot of writers, and when I start reading a spec, when I open up page one, "*Raymond* spec by Joey," I think, "I can't read this. It's painful." Because there's so many of them out there they all look the same. But when I read [an original script] and I watch this person develop a whole group of people and tell a story... that gives you a much better shot. The more original, the more unique your stuff is, the better, rather than trying to hit a certain place that's going to get you employed, [which] usually just makes you like everybody else."

READING PRODUCED SCREENPLAYS

You should read and analyze as many screenplays as possible, to see the good and the bad. The more you read, the more you detect patterns in structure and you build mental lists of what works and what doesn't.

It can be difficult to find produced screenplays in their original format. It's important to note that many published scripts found in bookstores are not in industry-standard format and most professional screenplays to be found online are production drafts, not spec submission drafts. Production drafts tend to run much longer (e.g., 120+ pages) than your average spec script, can be littered with camera and shot references and the style is often heightened as "actor-bait" to attract talent. This is just one of the reasons why it's so important to hunt down the actual drafts of produced screenplays and to show your work to your peers (and, ideally, also to professionals who've worked in the industry), to make sure it's formatted and written to flow as a "reader's draft."

[Note: I'm going to use examples from several produced screenplays in this section, and in each case I've done my best to replicate exactly the text of the script as printed. Many of my sample scripts were referenced from hard copies, but in the case of the downloaded screenplays, I cannot vouch for the accuracy of the transcription.]

CAPTURING THE MOMENT

Shane Black's *Lethal Weapon* screenplay [Warner Bros. Pictures, Silver Pictures] may be ancient history at this point, but at the time it had a huge impact on the industry, and rightfully so. It's dripping with voice, has tons of commentary and never lets up, for better and for worse. The "worse" would be the asides and commentary in description, which are best to avoid when you're a new writer. In the "better" category, Black shows his penchant for nailing the TONE of a room with some distinctive language on page 1...

```
PASTEL colors. Window walls. New wave
furniture tortured into weird shapes. It
looks like robots live here.
```

I like the furniture being "tortured into weird shapes," but for me that "robots" line hits the bull's-eye. We immediately know this is a chic, Hollywood condo owned by people with too much money and zero compassion for their fellow human beings. That's not necessarily *commentary* for me, that's just good description.

But a little bit later, he throws in a line that feels disassociated from the introduction of the Martin Riggs character (Mel Gibson).

```
Riggs smiles at him innocently. Strokes the
collie's fur with one hand.
```

```
With the other, he reaches into a paper sack
and produces, a spanking new bottle of Jack
Daniels, possibly the finest drink mankind
has yet produced.
```

That Jack Daniels line feels like it's trying too hard, doesn't it? Now, if I knew I was reading a Shane Black screenplay, since this type of aside is his calling card, I'd throw him a little slack.

But not you. The unknown. The newbie. You get no slack, scribe.

But you can do something about it. You remember.

You can be <u>elegant</u>...

...which by definition means *gracefully concise and simple; admirably succinct.*

Concise, simple, and succinct. Damn, I love those words. Why? Because they so rarely describe what I read! But I always <u>want</u> them to.

So that's your task.

Use as few words as possible.

But make them the BEST words.

Which, I know, can be crippling to you playwrights, novelists and poets who are used to waxing on like Mr. friggin' Miyagi with his backyard deck over here. But welcome to screenwriting. It's a totally different animal. And it thrives on simple, elegant prose.

You MUST learn to capture an entire mood in a single word or short line of dialogue. If you can't, then personally I don't think you have any business writing screenplays.

Why?

Because of the Reader. Remember that lovely gatekeeper of a human being? They, like the average filmgoer or channel surfer...don't...have... time...to...waste.

So keep it short. And sweet. And use --

white space. It's your friend.

And keep those description paragraphs to 2-4 lines thick. And by great Odin's beard make sure it's CLEAR. Show us what we see and what we hear in the most straightforward, clear way possible...while still choosing the best word in the entire English lexicon. No biggee, right?

Actually, it is. But to make you feel better, I've prepared some handy lists, which are always fun and never dull and are most often like having a cake and eating it too...

TO DO --

- **Be clear**
- **Be specific**
- **Be elegant**
- **Be unique** (without being too *literary*)
- **Use strong, active verbs**
- **Capture tone**

<u>NOT</u> TO DO --

- **Don't explain**
- **Don't comment**
- **Don't use forms of "be"** (*is, are*)
- **Don't use generic descriptions** (e.g. "He looks like the All-American captain of the football team.")

So those are the rules. And yes, they're broken all the time, sometimes in brilliant ways, but mostly in ham-handed ways. Here's an example of a nice break of the rules.

In *As Good as it Gets* [Tristar Pictures, Gracie Films], writers Mark Andrus and James L. Brooks "direct" the shot and comment all over the place, but they manage to beautifully capture the first kiss between MELVIN (Jack Nicholson) and CAROL (Helen Hunt):

Carol moves to the chair next to him... She sits very close -- he tenses.

> CAROL
> Have you ever let a romantic moment make you do something you know is stupid?

> MELVIN
> Never.

> CAROL
> Here's the trouble with never.

TIGHT SHOT

for the kiss. Their faces are close -- she looks at him... She closes her eyes -- her face moving toward him -- he is wide-eyed and afraid... His face almost moves away --

in a shot this close it's almost flight...
But now his head moves back and he receives
her kiss. It is brief. Carol smiles
encouragement to him and herself. Melvin
can't bear the pleasure.

                    MELVIN
          You don't owe me that.

If you lean back and look at that big paragraph as a whole, it
looks unwieldy with all the ellipses and dashes, but when
you read it...it works. And I can't say why, or how they did it.

That's for you to wonder. Have fun with that.

On the opposite end of the emotional and genre spectrum,
here's a brutal scene from the opening of an early draft of
Robert Rodat's *Saving Private Ryan* [Dreamworks SKG,
Paramount Pictures] that I found on the web...

THE LEAD LANDING CRAFT

The Motorman holds his course. Shells
EXPLODE around them. FLAMING OIL BURNS on
the water. CANNON FIRE SMASHES into the bow.

THE MOTORMAN IS RIPPED TO BITS

BLOOD AND FLESH shower the men behind him.
The MATE takes the controls.

A YOUNG SOLDIER

His face covered with the remains of the
motorman. Starts to lose it. Begins to
shudder and weep. His name is DELANCEY.

THE BOYS AROUND HIM

Do their best to stare straight ahead. But
the fear infects them. It starts to spread.

A FIGURE

Pushes through the men. Puts himself in front of DeLancey.

The figure is CAPTAIN JOHN MILLER. Early thirties. By far the oldest man on the craft. Relaxed, battle-hardened, powerful, ignoring the hell around them. He smiles, puts a cigar in his mouth, strikes a match on the front of DeLancey's helmet and lights the cigar.

Rodat immediately brings us into this deadly world. He starts out with a very intense voice to reflect the battle, creating an immediate sense of dread and chaos with the shells EXPLODING, canon fire, burning oil, and the Motorman being "RIPPED TO BITS." He uses very specific word choice and grammar...

His face covered with the remains of the motorman. Starts to lose it. Begins to shudder and weep. His name is DELANCEY.

Rodat avoids a conventional active sentence, such as "DeLancey, a 19 year old private, begins to shake and cry." That wouldn't be as interesting as the description "Starts to lose it. Begins to shudder and weep." which is shorter and thus reads more intensely. The introduction of the man's name at the end of the paragraph adds an edge as well. Then we meet the men...

Do their best to stare straight ahead. But the fear infects them. It starts to spread.

Can "fear spreading" be shown or is this a breaking of the rules, a telling of something internal? It's a bit of both, but it works, in that we can picture the fear as these boys all adopt terrified looks on their faces. It's elegant and economical, so he doesn't need to show us three or four specific soldiers and what they're doing (e.g., crying, knuckles going white on rifles, praying, etc.). He lets us picture it in our head as we will, but he manages to capture the TONE—fear and foreboding. We've been dropped with these men into a nightmare. And it's just beginning— something's coming and it will no doubt be deadly.

NICE TO MEET ME

```
A FIGURE

Pushes through the men. Puts himself in
front of DeLancey.
```

In the above description, Rodat chooses to introduce Miller (Tom Hanks) first as A FIGURE. This makes us picture his back, assuming his face can't be seen by the camera. And it gives a sense that he is a dark character, to be feared; maybe he's in charge of this mess? Then when he strikes his match on DeLancey's helmet and lights up a cigar in the midst of this hellish scenario, we are shown his character through action: he's a seasoned, tough-as-nails veteran of war who refuses to succumb to fear.

Notice how he <u>Puts himself in front of DeLancey</u>; he doesn't "stand" in front of him or "address" him. This is a man who will throw his body in front of *anything*, and this shows even more in the next scene as he enters the fray and fights with reckless abandon.

Here's Stuart Beattie's introduction of VINCENT (Tom Cruise) in his screenplay *Collateral* [Paramount Pictures], page 1...

```
FADE IN:

INT. BRADLEY TERMINAL - BLURS - DAY

slide past in a 400mm lens. Then, entering a
plane of focus is VINCENT. He walks towards
us...an arriving passenger.

Suit. Shirt. Tie. Sunglasses and expensive
briefcase say "confident executive
```

traveler." The suit's custom-made but not
domestic.

His hair and shades are current, but it
would be difficult to describe his
identifying specifics...grey suit, white
shirt, medium height. And that's the idea...

The little commentary blurb "And that's the idea..." clues us
into the scenario, draws us into what seems to be a ruse, a
disguise of some sort. Some game is being played. We don't
yet know if it's a funny or deadly game, but we'll soon find
out.

I especially like that the description and commentary are not
describing anything internal; it's all <u>shown</u>.

Unlike this example, which unfortunately comes from *As
Good as it Gets,* and if it were in a spec from a newbie I'd file
it under the NOT TO DO column...

MELVIN UDALL

in the hallway... Well past 50... unliked,
unloved, unsettling. A huge pain in the ass
to everyone he's ever met. Right now all his
considerable talent and strength is totally
focused on seducing a tiny dog into the
elevator door he holds open.

This description TELLS us about this guy, it EXPLAINS him to
us. Which might be fine, if he weren't about to SHOW us he's
devoid of love and a huge pain in the ass to everyone he
meets, starting with the detestable yet hilarious act of
shoving that tiny dog down the trash chute!

Next, we see him perform the following actions, which I
would file under the TO DO column...

```
INT. MELVIN'S APARTMENT, BATHROOM - NIGHT

Melvin locks and unlocks and locks his door,
counting to five with each lock.

He turns the lights quickly on and off and
on five times and makes a straight-line
towards his bathroom where he turns on the
hot water and opens the medicine chest.

INT. MEDICINE CHEST

Scores of neatly stacked Neutrogena soaps.
He unwraps one -- begins to wash -- discards
it -- goes through the process two more
times.
```

Nice details.

Here's the introduction of LT. DAN from *Forrest Gump* by Eric Roth [Based on the novel by Winston Groom; Paramount Pictures]. Roth chooses to use very little description, letting the dialogue and actions speak for him...

```
Lieutenant DAN TAYLOR steps out of a tent.
Shirtless, he holds a roll of toilet paper
in his hand.

                    LT. DAN
          You must be my F.N.G.'s.


                    BUBBA AND FORREST
          Morning, sir!


                    LT. DAN
          Ho! Get your hands down. Do not
          salute me. There are goddamned
          snipers all around this area who
          would love to grease an officer.
```

                    I'm Lieutenant Dan Taylor.
                    Welcome to Fourth Platoon.

         Lt. Dan looks at Bubba.

                              LT. DAN
                    What's wrong with your lips?

                              BUBBA
                    I was born with big gums, sir.

                              LT. DAN
                    Yeah, well, you better tuck that in.
                    Gonna get that caught on a trip
         wire.
                    Where you boys from in the world?

                           BUBBA & FORREST
                    Alabama, sir!

                              LT. DAN
                    You twins?

         Forrest and Bubba look at each other oddly,
         they don't get the joke.

                              FORREST
                    No, we are not relations, sir.

Concise and funny, it works.

Here, the screenwriters of *The Chronicles of Narnia: The
Lion, The Witch and the Wardrobe* [Ann Peacock and Andrew
Adamson and Christopher Markus & Stephen McFeely, Based
on the book by C.S. Lewis; Walt Disney Pictures, Walden
Media] manage to achieve a nice sense of wonder...

The Centaur stares at him, unmoving.

                    PETER
          We...have come to see...Aslan.

The centaur says nothing.

Suddenly behind them all of the creatures
kneel, leaving the three Pevensies standing
alone.

Peter blinks. Suddenly, LUCY GASPS.

Just below the tent flap steps...an ENORMOUS
PAW.

The flap parts, and there in the shining
sunlight stands a

FEARSOME, BEAUTIFUL, GOLDEN...

LION. He gazes at them. His mane shimmers.

Lucy stares for a moment...then KNEELS. The
Beavers drop to all fours, bowing their
heads.

Peter and Susan awkwardly go down on one
knee.

Aslan addresses the CHILDREN in a BOOMING
VOICE.

                    ASLAN
          Welcome, Peter, Son of Adam.
          Welcome, Susan and Lucy, Daughters
          of Eve.

Another. Completely different feel. From *American History X*,
by David McKenna [New Line Cinema]...

TIGHT ON DEREK VINYARD. The young man has a
shaved head, a trimmed goatee, and a
SWASTIKA on his right tit -- the center of
the symbol crossed perfectly at the nipple.

McKenna calls a man's chest a "tit." It gives an edge, an
intensity, a *street* feel to this young man. And you notice he
puts swastika in CAPS, because it's such a strong image and
it immediately and dramatically introduces the themes of
white supremacy and hatred that will permeate the story.
This demonstrates the need for you to...

BE SPECIFIC

Sometimes it's just one distinctive word or phrase that
brings the zing.

In *Collateral*, Stuart Beattie calls Vincent's gun by its dealer
name: PARA-ORDNANCE. An unwieldy term to be sure, much
more so than just "pistol" or ".45," but distinctive and
memorable and it makes the writer sound like he really
knows what he's talking about. After the first couple times
we read it, our eye skips over it and the text flows faster.

VINCENT APPEARS

around a corner, clearing space. Fast. His
Para-Ordnance up.

Max and Annie running, now... Vincent sees
vague shapes...

BOOM-BOOM! BOOM-BOOM! Gunshots punch through
the glass, inches from Max and Annie,
collapsing walls revealing Vincent against
the LA-scape.

Blossoms of white flame: BOOM-BOOM...

*Clearing space...collapsing walls...blossoms of white
flame*...very nice word choice.

William Monahan uses the adjective "flash" several times in *The Departed*, to denote the contrast between the rich upper-crust world that Colin (Matt Damon) aspires to and the filthy underbelly that he must cater to, as here on page 20...

```
INT. APARTMENT ON BEACON HILL - TWILIGHT

A REALTOR switches on lights. An empty,
flash apartment above

the Parisian rooftops of Beacon Hill. A view
of the Dome.

More than you'd think a cop could afford.
```

On page 8, Monahan comes up with a clever linguistic take on a generic tension device as BILLY (Leonardo DiCaprio) takes the police exam...

```
A CLOCK TICKS, sweep hand coming around.

BILLY'S EYES on it.
```

I love that "sweep hand" term. Never seen it. And I like how he didn't bother with the CLOSE ON Billy's eyes, he just showed us BILLY'S EYES, so naturally we view this shot in our minds eye in Close Up. We don't need the "direction."

Here's a lusty moment from *Casanova* [Screenplay by Jeffrey Hatcher and Kimberly Simi; Touchstone Pictures] page 4 of the production draft...

```
                    DIFFERENT WOMAN
          My husband!

Casanova runs into a dark closet. The
darkness becomes the interior of a covered
gondola.

We pull away and see the boat floating in a
canal-- legs sticking out from all sides
from under the felze.
```

What in the name of Caravaggio is "felze?" I have no idea, but it sounds like something they'd have in Venice in 1797, so I'm on board with it.

Let's look at a quick moment from Wes Anderson and Owen Wilson's *Rushmore* [Touchstone Pictures]...

```
Mr. Fischer holds up a hand mirror so Gordon
can see the back. Gordon nods.

Max comes in rolling a Japanese ten-speed at
his side.
```

The phrase "rolling a Japanese ten-speed at his side" adds so much more color than flat blocking like "Max walks in with his bike," or leaving out the bike with simply "Max enters." The reference to the Japanese ten-speed says, "this is a kid" and, "remember when you had a Fuji ten-speed?" It's a connection the author makes with you.

```
Max looks across the yard at MAGNUS BUCHAN,
the burly foreign-exchange student from
Scotland. He is seventeen. He has a straw in
his mouth, and he shoots a small blowdart at
a little kid's neck.

Half of Buchan's ear was blown off in a
hunting accident.
```

We never know from watching the film how Buchan's ear became deformed. But in mentioning it to the reader in a line of what amounts to commentary (normally a "no-no,"), the authors clue us in to this character's motivations and emotional makeup. We not only see him shooting a blowdart at a little kid, but we now know why he does this kind of thing. He's an angry bully. An interesting one. A unique one. Not because he shoots a blowdart at a helpless victim (although that's certainly more interesting than, say, punching a kid in the arm), but because half of his ear (not his whole ear, *half*) was blown off in a hunting accident.

Now, if one of us were to write that line, we may have written the cause of his deformity as an accident with fireworks. But that would have been wrong. The "hunting accident" makes us picture a domineering father, a macho insecure factor, maybe an abusive home—when we watch the film we SEE Buchan represents these types of traits due to the actor's performance. But on paper the actor is not present, so the writers compensate with compelling prose. The words fill in for the performance.

WE GET IT

Unfortunately, even the pros exhibit the bad habit of explaining too much in their production drafts, but we'll let them slide because they may be catering to the skimming habits of all of the execs, actors and crew members who will be reading this draft.

In this excerpt from *Collateral*, I've bolded the offending line for your reading pleasure...

VINCENT + MAX

sit there, riding the train. Softly:

                    MAX
          We're almost at the next stop.

Vincent smiles faintly. He leans his head toward Max as if conferring a secret. In a halting whisper:

                    VINCENT
          Hey, Max... A guy gets on the MTA
          here in LA and dies.
                    (off Max's look)
          Think anybody...will notice?

MAX

looks into Vincent's eyes. **It means "I'm
that guy" and "will anybody notice that
once...I was here?"**

VINCENT

leans back, gazing straight ahead now.
Rocking gently with the motion of the train.
And then Vincent's no longer rocking. In
fact, Vincent's no longer doing anything.
Ever.

We know what Vincent means, and we get the call back to
the first exchange between him and Max in the opening
pages. No need to point it out. It's especially extraneous,
considering this elegant moment on the last page of the
script, the last we'll ever see of Vincent the assassin...

WE HOLD ON Vincent for awhile. Riding the
train by himself, his head forward as if
sleeping, alone in the car.

Another dead guy on the subway...riding
somewhere.

I will concede that commentary often works for historical or
culturally complicated pieces, to provide facts to the reader.

For example, Stephen Gaghan's *Syriana* [Warner Bros.
Pictures, Participant Productions]...

INT GROTTO - BEIRUT - DAY

An ancient grotto where the early Christians
used to hide, be discovered, and executed. A
tourist attraction, it's a cool, vast, dimly
lit, subterranean space.

I'll leave it up to you to decide if that little history of the
grotto aids the script or not. If one considers that the goal
with submission was to find a producer interested in the

Middle East, then I'd warrant it was appreciated. But too many of these asides would quickly make the script into a history lesson, an excuse for an amateur writer to show off their research.

Here are a couple more excerpts from *The Departed*, what I'd label good and bad.

Here, Monahan toes the line of explanation and showing...

>   YOUNG COSTELLO
>   Church wants you in your place.
>   Do this don't do that, kneel, stand,
>   kneel, stand...I mean if you go for
>   that sort of thing...
>
> YOUNG COLIN, the recent altar boy, visibly
> *doesn't* go for that sort of thing.

...and it works. But next, this parenthetical is in dire need of a red pen!

>   COLIN
>   (not vainglorious, but
>   innocently stretching for
>   the idea)
>   You're in trouble if you're "only"
>   anything.

Not vainglorious? *Innocently stretching*? Will these terms be on the test, Professor Abercrombie Yoshihiro?

PACE YOURSELF

There are different methods for capturing those moments when the pulse must race. Here's an example of an action sequence from Tony Kushner and Eric Roth's screenplay *Munich* [Based on the Book "Vengeance" by George Jonas.

Dreamworks SKG, Universal Pictures]. It's dynamic and it flows well, but with no CAPPING, it certainly feels different than a thriller like *Collateral*. Softer, perhaps? Was this intentional, since *Munich* is a historical drama?

Avner leans further in. He can just see the foot of the bed, and al-Chir's legs sliding under the bedclothes. He lowers himself back to his own balcony, goes in his room, switches off the light.

A beat, and then an enormous explosion; the wall Avner's room shares with al-Chir's is pushed in and falls over, intact, knocking Avner back onto his bed.

The fan in the ceiling above is sheared off and falls, nearly hitting Avner.

EXT. THE HOTEL OLYMPIC - NIGHT

Smoke and flames explode from al-Chir's room across his balcony.

EXT. THE STREET IN FRONT OF THE HOTEL OLYMPIC - NIGHT

Glass and plaster and stone rain down on the street, bouncing off a car in which Steve and Carl are sitting.

Seems a bit odd that they wouldn't cap an "enormous explosion," doesn't it? Just for the sake of research, let's look at another Eric Roth action scene, from *Forrest Gump*...

Forrest looks up as the sun suddenly appears. Forrest's platoon is attacked. A bullet kills the soldier standing next to Forrest. Bombs explode all around as the soldiers scramble to the ground.

                        LT. DAN
            Take cover!

Forrest crawls over a berm as bullets fly
overhead and explode all around him.

Yeah, I think it's safe to say that Eric Roth doesn't like CAPS...but
I'm not going to argue with the writer of *Forrest Gump, The Insider*
and *Ali* so we'll call it even.

XVI. DIALOGUE

As you can no doubt surmise by now with my "lean and mean" philosophy, I don't think your characters need to talk like they just stepped out of a David Mamet or Quentin Tarantino film. A writer doesn't have to find startlingly original voices that have never been heard on film before; as long as there is CONTRAST in the voices so we can tell them apart, you'll do fine, and the more you write, the stronger your dialogue will become.

Dialogue is best when it's kept short, to the point, with no wasted words. Speaking of Tarantino, here's one of my favorite exchanges from *Pulp Fiction* [Miramax Films] — Butch the boxer (Bruce Willis) orders cigarettes from a Bartender:

                    BUTCH
          Pack of Red Apples.

                    BARTENDER
          Filters?

                    BUTCH
          None.

This punchy exchange replaces what could have been a flat, functional exchange.

A classic from *As Good As It Gets*:

                    RECEPTIONIST
          How do you write women so well?

                    MELVIN
          I take a man, and I remove reason
          and accountability.

Here's one from *Million Dollar Baby [screenplay by Paul Haggis, based on stories by F.X. Toole; Warner Bros. Pictures, Lakeshore Entertainment]*:

                    MAGGIE
          People say I'm pretty tough.

                    FRANKIE
          Girly, tough ain't enough.

And a great one from *Pirates of the Caribbean: The Curse of the Black Pearl [screenplay by Ted Elliot & Terry Rossio; screen story by T&T and Stuart Beattie and Jay Wolpert; Walt Disney Pictures]*:

                    NORRINGTON
          You are, without doubt, the worst
          pirate I've ever heard of.

                    JACK SPARROW
          But you *have* heard of me.

It's great every now and then to have a dramatic SPEECH by your main character (some writers call these "actor bait"), but try to keep them short and make sure this person's really got something to say:

                    MAGGIE
          Truth is, my brother's in
          prison. My sister cheats on
          welfare by pretending one of
          her babies is still alive.
          My daddy's dead and my mama
          weighs 312 pounds.
                    (MORE)

```
              MAGGIE (CONT.)
      If I was thinking straight, I'd
      go back home, find a used
      trailer, buy a deep fryer and
      some Oreo's. Problem is, this is
      the only thing I ever felt good
      doin'.
```

A new writer would do themselves well to keep it simple and focused. But, unfortunately, too many succumb to the dark side and we get lots of new writers that think their dialogue is unique, snappy, and explodes off the page when it's really just an unmotivated rip-off of one of their favorite movies. I say *unmotivated* because I often read characters in scripts who talk like multi-cultural, autistic savant pimps...but they're supposed to be small-town accountants and housewives!

Perhaps I'm exaggerating a bit, but the point is we must believe that these people would speak like this, and you must keep it consistent and truthful to the logical world that you have created. Notice how everyone in *Pulp Fiction* has a very distinctive way of speaking, in a way that no normal person would speak. It's a highly stylized 'world' that they live in. Tarantino keeps it consistent, so we buy it.

Now if his two dark-suited hitmen, Jules and Vincent, walked into, say, *American Beauty*, something would be a bit amiss. Because their speech would not be consistent with the world of the characters in Alan Ball's script. But yet in that film, we believe the teenager Ricky Fitts speaks in a poetic style because he's been established as a withdrawn, artistic type of character. It makes sense. He may not speak like any teenage boy you know, but that's okay, because...MOVIES ARE NOT REAL LIFE. People don't talk in movies like they do in real life—they couldn't—it would prove tedious for an audience. All the stops and starts, the pointless observations, the information left out because the other person already knows it; this would confuse an audience. As Hemingway said...

"Good dialogue is not real speech, it is the ILLUSION of real speech."

We may think the characters in a script talk like real people we know, but maybe that's just us feeling real emotion that was stirred in us by the dialogue. Which is a wonderful thing and your goal—to be able to make a reader or viewer feel the emotions that your characters are feeling.

Easier said than done. But that's why we're here. Let's look at some guidelines for dialogue I've laid out.

GOOD DIALOGUE:

a) Moves the story forward.

b) Reveals crucial character.

c) Explores theme in a unique manner.

d) Feels motivated.

e) Avoids cliché phrases.

MANY GOOD DIALOGUE SCENES:

a) Have a beginning, middle, and end.

b) Place characters in a location of external conflict (e.g., in a taxi cab, on line at the deli) rather than just a static location (e.g., sitting at a table in a restaurant, on the phone).

c) Subvert our expectations (i.e. Take surprising turns).

d) End with a surprising/humorous turnabout.

e) Characters talk *around* the subject, not directly to it (aka "on the nose" dialogue).

f) Characters show themselves to us through their reactions, they don't tell us exactly how they feel.

g) Characters acknowledge and react to the subtext of the scene.

The final, and sometimes best, thing a good dialogue scene can do is...

SET UP A MONEY LINE!

I love it when a scene sets up a <u>money line</u> and then delivers on it.

Think of Jack Nicholson for inspiration:

- "You can't handle the truth!"

- "Here's Johnny!"

- "Wait'll they get a load of me."

Here's a famous scene from *As Good As It Gets*. Carol and Melvin go on their first proper date, and Melvin unwittingly insults her. She demands he pay her a compliment (note: the bold emphasis is mine)...

```
                MELVIN
     My compliment is that when you came
     to my house that time and told me
     how you'd never -- well, you were
     there, you know... The next
     morning I started taking these
     pills.
```

                    CAROL
               (a little confused)
          I don't quite get how that's a
          compliment for me.

Amazing that something in Melvin rises to
the occasion -- so that he
uncharacteristically looks at her directly -
- then:

                    MELVIN
          **You make me want to be a better
          man.**

Carol never expected the kind of praise
which would so slip under her guard. She
stumbles a bit -- flattered, momentarily
moved and his for the taking.

                    CAROL
          That's maybe the best compliment
          of my life.

                    MELVIN
          Then I've really overshot here
          'cause I was aiming at just enough
          to keep you from walking out.

Carol laughs.

Hustle & Flow is about a wanna-be rapper preparing to
hustle the one guy who made it out of their poor town, a
successful rapper named Skinny Black — the big confrontation
comes at the end of Act Two, when DJay hooks Skinny Black
with a brilliant hustle, culminating in a sweet money line...

D.Jay removes an old cassette tape and
slides it across the table to Skinny Black.

Skinny looks down to see his old underground
tape. He colored his own name like a
graffiti tag. It is over a decade old.
Skinny carefully picks it up and, to the
wonder of all, removes his shades.

> SKINNY BLACK
> My underground. Look, Tigga.
> Slobs, look at what this nigga
> got.
>> (genuine)
> I... can't believe you got one
> of these, man. I don't got none
> of these left.

> D.JAY
>> (leans in for effect)
> **Skinny, you got thousands of
> these in you.** Just come back home.

Everyone is silent. They all look to Skinny
Black.

In *City Slickers*, Phil (Daniel Stern) asks his friends "What's
the best and worst day of your life?"

Mitch (Billy Crystal) says his first Yankees game at age 7 and
the day his wife found a lump in her breast.

Phil says his wedding day and every day since.

Ed (Bruno Kirby) tells the sad story of the day when he was
14 and his mother caught his father cheating. Ed kicked his
father out and he became the man of the house.

The scene ends with this exchange...

```
                    ED
I took care of my mother and
my sister from that day on.
That's my best day.

                   PHIL
What was your worst day?

                    ED
```
Same day.

This is a textbook "button" — that perfect final line to end a scene in style.

DIALOGUE SCENES CHART

I think it was Paddy Chayefsky who said "Everybody loves a good chart."

GOOD	BAD
The "Illusion Of Real Speech"	Real Speech
Showing	Telling
Beginning, Middle, End	Rambling
Builds to GOAL of Scene	Static; No Urgency
Escalating Conflict	Lack of New Conflict
External Conflicts (location, weather, time,)	"Talking Heads" (static, seated)
Motivated, Logical	Poetry for its own sake

GOOD	BAD
Unique Word Choice	Generic Word Choice
Talking "around" the Topic	Direct "Reporting" on the Topic
Reactions to events shown	Direct Comments about Offscreen events
Using Subtext	Explaining Subtext
Surprise	Predictable
What do they want from the other?	Unclear Goals
What's at Stake?	No Consequences
Reveals Unique Character	Adheres to Basic Characterization (stock features)

BOGARTIN' BUKOWSKI

Here's a scene from *Sideways* with some nice details. Jack, the eternally hopeful one, is trying to cheer up his depressive friend Miles after Miles' book was rejected.

EXT. BEACH - DAY

Two PELICANS soar low over the water. One of them DIVES, crashing into the water and disappearing from view.

Jack and Miles sit on the hood of the Saab, gazing at the ocean, sharing a bottle of wine.

                    JACK
Just write another one. You have
lots of ideas, right?

                    MILES
No, I'm finished. I'm not a
writer. I'm a middle-school
English teacher. I'm going to
spend the rest of my life grading
essays and reading the work of
others. It's okay. I like books.
The world doesn't give a shit what
I have to say. I'm unnecessary.
 (a dark laugh)
I'm so insignificant, I can't even
kill myself.

                    JACK
What's that supposed to mean?

                    MILES
You know -- Hemingway, Sexton,
Woolf, Plath, Delmore Schwartz.
You can't even kill yourself before
you've even published.

                    JACK
What about that guy who wrote
Confederacy of Dunces? He
committed suicide before he got
published, and look how famous he
is.

                    MILES
          Thanks.

                    JACK
          Don't give up. You're going to
          make it.

                    MILES
          Half my life is over, and I have
          nothing to show for it. I'm a
          thumbprint on the window of a
          skyscraper. I'm a smudge of
          excrement on a tissue surging out
          to sea with a million tons of raw
          sewage.

                    JACK
          See? Right there. Just what you
          just said. That's beautiful. A
          thumbprint on a skyscraper. I
          couldn't write that.

                    MILES
          Neither could I. I think it's
          Bukowski.

Unable to respond, Jack looks up and down
the beach.

JUNO WHAT I'M SAYIN'?

Here's a fun scene from *Juno* where we really get a sense of
the different voices of the characters.

INT. LORING HOUSE - LIVING ROOM - DAY

Mark and Vanessa usher Juno and Mac into the austere, spacious living room. A woman in a business suit sits on the couch with a briefcase in her lap.

                    MARK
          This is our attorney, Gerta Rauss.

                    JUNO
               (in exaggerated, growling
               German accent)
          Geeeeerta Rauuuss!

                    GERTA
               (straight)
          Nice to meet you.

Mac seizes Mark's hand and pumps it heartily.

                    MAC
          I'm Mac MacGuff, and this, of
          course, is my daughter Juno.

                    MARK
          Like the city in Alaska?

                    JUNO
          No.

                    MARK
          Cool. Well, let's sit down and get
          to know each other a bit.

>   VANESSA
> I'll get drinks. What would everyone
> like? I've got Pellegrino, Vitamin
> Water...

>   JUNO
> A Maker's Mark, please. Up.

>   MAC
> She's joking. Junebug has a
> wonderful sense of humor, which is
> just one of her many genetic gifts.

>   JUNO
> I also have good teeth. No
> cavities. We finally got
> fluoridated water in Dancing Elk.

She bares them frighteningly to demonstrate.

Vanessa stares, unflappable.

VOICE-OVER

I'm not a fan.

I'm not a fan because it's rare that it's truly crucial to the reader's understanding of the story, so it's often used as a story crutch to impart exposition.

I also feel that it's most often limp on the page. Without hearing the actor's voice deliver the narration, it just doesn't hold much power.

Try to imagine these three great voice-overs without the inflection of the actors:

- Ray Liotta as Henry Hill in *Goodfellas*.

- Morgan Freeman as Red in *The Shawshank Redemption*.

- Sam Elliott as The Stranger in *The Big Lebowski*

I'd argue that they would read flat and excessive on the page.

Bottom line, if you're going to use Voiceover, it must be specific, vital and advance the story. Or just plain fun.

I encourage you to do something different with it. For example, in the movie *Little Children*, the Voiceover is delivered by the voice actor that narrates all those nature and history documentaries on cable. His dialogue is written in the style of an ethnographic piece, treating the subjects in the story as if they were animals on the savannah in Africa.

In *Million Dollar Baby*, Morgan Freeman's narration imparts a crucial setup when he tells us about the fighter known as The Blue Bear: "She didn't know that could kill a person." This motivates the punch that she inflicts on Maggie, breaking her neck.

In *There Will Be Blood*, Daniel Plainview (Daniel Day Lewis) pitches his oil company to the townsfolk who must approve the drilling of a new well. His speech continues in voice-over as we flash-forward to see shots of the camp that he will eventually build. These shots show us that he's lying to the townspeople. By compressing time and using a contrast between dialogue and visuals, we've been shown crucial character development and advanced the story.

XVII. CHARACTER

No one can tell you exactly how to create a compelling dramatic character that a reader and audience will identify with and care about, nor can they tell you if your screenplay should initially flow from that character or from the plot, but I can suggest certain guidelines and characteristics that may aid you in writing characters that feel real and fleshed-out for the 110 pages we will spend with them.

The most important thing to heed:

CHARACTER = ACTION

Give your characters unique actions and decisions. SHOW their character, who they are, how they feel and how they view the world, through their actions. Dialogue is also vital to establishing a unique character, but actions are *more* important.

Character, to me, is rather simple. More often than not it should be logical, motivated and consistent. Most of the time in a film we don't have time to continually develop new facets of a person's character, revealing sides of them that are complex and contradictory. It's possible, but it's tough to work into a tightly plotted story. There's only so much room for growth, so I would suggest targeting the signpost beats for these moments of change in your characters, especially with your Protagonist, whose development, or "arc," is the most important. (By the way, if you're wondering which of your characters is the true Protagonist, it's usually the one who goes through the most change).

FROM THE TRENCHES:

"<u>Character</u>. We're always looking to hire writers who can put great characters into one of our current screenplays in development, in *all genres*."

The Lesson: Every screenplay, regardless of genre or style, needs memorable characters. Strong character skills will increase your worth as a writer in the industry, especially with open writing assignments (where you are hired to rewrite a purchased screenplay).

Strong, believable motivation for a character's actions is crucial. We demand stronger motivation from a script than from a film. On film, contradictions are easier to handle because you're seeing this charismatic actor do these things and there's no way to change it. But a script is malleable; you can always just change that little bit that doesn't work for you, so the writer needs to work harder on earning those beats.

Miles Raymond in *Sideways* is really stealing $800 from his mother's sock drawer; Mr. Blonde in *Reservoir Dogs* really is cutting the cop's ear off; William Wallace in *Braveheart*

FROM THE TRENCHES:

Vincent Kartheiser (Peter Campbell on *Mad Men*)

At the season four premiere of the brilliant television drama *Mad Men*, I asked actor Vincent Kartheiser what he looks for in a great script. He said, **"Character. I want to see a story about real people."**

The Lesson: Actors are often THE factor that gets a script made into a movie. And what are actors looking for? **Great characters, ripped from real life, not other movies.**

really is making love to the French princess even though less than a year ago his beloved wife was murdered by minions of the princess' father-in-law, the British King. If we had read these things on the page we might have said "baloney, he'd never do that!" But we see these actors on screen and we like them, so we pretty much buy whatever they do (within reason).

But your script does not have the benefit of movie stars!

I'm not saying don't make your characters complex or contradictory in any way; after all, we as human beings possess contradictions in our character and film should reflect the human condition. Just keep it focused and motivated, and respect that it's hard to get a Reader to go along with too many turns in a character's motivation and essential makeup. At your level, I think you should always lean toward focus and simplicity.

Most of what you need to establish your protagonist can be found in your Basic Story Map:

Age, basic physical description, occupation, External and Internal Goal, Skill, and Misbehavior.

That's it! We don't need to know a complete backstory on any character in your entire story. Whether you include one is up to you, but I think you'd probably be better off not worrying about the details of their life history and focusing on NOW. Their needs, goals, and conflicts NOW.

SYMPATHY

Too many films these days focus on an anti-hero with very few, if any, redeeming qualities. It's okay to have a protagonist with a dark side, but if they're ALL dark, it's going to be tough for us to root for them. At the least, they need some kind of a moral core. Some code of justice that they adhere to.

Too often, I see films that rely too much on extreme minimalism — we're thrown into the story without any background on the main character, so we're left to struggle to figure out the crucial Basic Story Map elements. (Examples of protagonists that I found lacking are in *Animal Kingdom, Syriana* and *Michael Clayton*.)

The three most simple ways to gain our sympathy for your protagonist:

- Show them doing the right thing, early on. If they help another human being, or even an animal, it shows they have a heart.

- Give them justice on their side. They can be chopping off heads left and right, but if they're on a righteous quest, we'll root for them.

- Make the bad guy <u>worse</u>! Simple as that. In *Sideways*, Miles is a pompous, depressive complainer, but Jack is a tier-one asshole so Miles is the one we root for. In *American Beauty*, the lustful Lester fantasizes about a 16 year-old girl. But his wife is worse: she's screwing the king of real estate!

In *The Informant*, Matt Damon's protagonist is a dolt who is playing everyone. But the problem is, we never see the smart guy; we only see the doofus. Also, we're never shown a reason to trust him, so the big reveal doesn't work; when we find out he's been lying about everything, it's not that big of a deal because we never thought he *wasn't* lying. It could have gone either way, because this guy was so freakin' weird! Unlike other films, like *Primal Fear* or *The Usual Suspects*, *The Informant* didn't establish goals and attributes that pulled us in the other direction, so when they moved it to the true direction it didn't have the impact they intended.

More Matt Damon...

Sometimes we just need more <u>context</u> so we can figure out how to feel about a character. In *Syriana*, Matt Damon's character spends the film yelling about the corroding infrastructure of Saudi Arabia. He's OUTRAGED about the corroding infrastructure of Saudi Arabia! But...there's no reason for us to care about the corroding infrastructure of Saudi Arabia because it's never shown.

Even more Matt Damon...

We DO care about his character Jason Bourne, because he's not only on a righteous quest (to find out who he is) but he also *has incredible skills*. He's an amazing bad-ass when it comes to martial arts and espionage. There's that level of wish fulfillment that generates an emotional connection with those amazing fighters, like Leonidas in *300* or Lara Croft in *Tomb Raider*. Then there's the "genius quotient," which can instantly generate rooting interest in protagonists like John Nash in *A Beautiful Mind*, Mark Zuckerberg in *The Social Network* or Julia Child in *Julie & Julia*. If they're <u>the best</u> at what they do, there's a good chance we'll root for them, even if they're a villain like Hans Gruber in *Die Hard*.

Or if they're Matt Damon...in *Good Will Hunting*. What is it with this guy?!

In *Quills*, I never rooted for Geoffrey Rush's Marquis de Sade as he wrote trashy novels from his prison cell, precisely because he wasn't a good writer — he wrote trash! It wasn't urgent that this guy get out of jail because his work wasn't serving any serious purpose; it was simply pabulum for the masses. The film was an interesting portrait of the obsessive artist and it wasn't afraid to push to extremes, but I never emotionally connected with or rooted for the protagonist, so the story didn't work for me.

Speaking of characters we hate (and by "we" I mean me), I can't help but think of *Babel*, which begs the question: what the frick are Brad Pitt and Cate Blanchett doing in Morocco? Who ARE these people and why should I care about them?! She gets shot and he's struggling to save her life, which is sad and (sort of) tense, but I never made any kind of emotional connection with either of them so I felt like I was just watching a bunch of hand-wringing by people I don't know.

SUPPORTING CHARACTERS

In the case of supporting characters, unless they have a strong line of action and an arc that must pay off, all you really need is to answer the question...WHAT DO THEY WANT?

Okay, it's also helpful to define a misbehavior for your supporting characters, but that may flow right from their main need or desire, which is what they

FROM THE TRENCHES:

PHILIP CHARLES MACKENZIE
(Actor/Director: Dog Day Afternoon, Roseanne, Frasier, Attention Shoppers)

"Actors want to see complexity in their characters on the page. People are inconsistent and contradictory, so why shouldn't dramatic characters be?"

want from this dramatic situation. If all they want is cheese, then that's pretty much their desire and their misbehavior. They're the "cheese guy." But enough about my life. (Hey, where's my rim shot?!)

Let's make this a rule...

If you know what a character wants in a scene, you will always know what they would do and say.

Thus...

You should always know what every character wants in any scene.

Do you? If your characters are just sitting in a coffee shop, chatting away about their college days, and this scene only exists for you to establish how they know each other and they don't really WANT anything from the other person- then guess what? It can probably be cut. Give us <u>stakes</u>. You want to avoid any material that only exists to establish, to set up, to explain, and to transition into another scene. Avoid the static "Talking Heads" scenes and the characters TELLING us directly about themselves.

But most of all, remember the first tenet of cinematic characters...

SHOW CHARACTER THROUGH ACTION

We learn much more about Melvin Udall (Jack Nicholson) in the opening of *As Good As It Gets* when he stuffs his neighbor's dog down a trash chute and goes through his obsessive-compulsive rituals than if we opened on him delivering a two-page monologue telling us his life story.

Butch (Bruce Willis) in *Pulp Fiction* chooses the samurai sword as his weapon, even when surrounded by hundreds of weapons in the pawn shop.

Maggie Fitzgerald (Hilary Swank) in *Million Dollar Baby* works as a waitress; she wraps a customer's left-over pork chop in tinfoil, lies to her boss that it's for her dog, then later we see her eating it for her dinner.

To use an earlier example, in *The Godfather*, Michael Corleone (Al Pacino) sips his cappuccino before shooting his target. This not only builds tension but shows us the hidden strength he possesses that will give credibility to his ascension to Don of the crime family.

In *Annie Hall*, Woody Allen's neurotic New Yorker and fish-out-of-water Alvy Singer sneezes into the pile of cocaine he's offered at a Hollywood party.

In *Seinfeld*, George Costanza and his fiancé Susan are looking at wedding invitation samples in a stationery store. The clerk tells them that the binder is organized with the most expensive in the front and the least expensive in the back. Without missing a beat...George turns to the back.

In *Rocky*, Rocky Balboa (Sylvester Stallone) shakes down a gambler but can't break the guy's thumbs like his boss told him to do. He's just too nice of a guy, and that's why we love him.

FROM THE TRENCHES:

MEETING ANTWONE FISHER
(*Antwone Fisher, ATL*)

I approached Antwone Fisher at an industry event and before I could say anything, he said to me **"Everybody hates agents. But you need them."**

It was a nice reminder that even though you're an artist, you need to accept and learn to deal with the necessities of the business side of your art.

He also told me about several un-produced specs he sold and assignments he'd worked, some worth millions of dollars, since he is a sought-after writer even though he only has a few produced credits. This highlighted how there are many screenwriters that are not known to the public, but well-respected in the industry and making comfortable livings.

THE CAREER

FROM THE TRENCHES:

BLUFFING MY WAY INTO
A PHONE CALL WITH
A MAJOR MANAGER

I set up a coffee meeting with a screenwriter that I met online, a guy who had a couple movies produced by the Sci-Fi Channel, at the trendy *Urth Caffe* in West Hollywood (the place that I've had the most celebrity sightings, including Lindsey Lohan, Conan O'Brien, Sarah Silverman and Alanis Morissette). Let's say this writer's name was Jim Salinger. I'd never met him in person so he emailed me a short description of his appearance.

I was sitting on the patio looking around, waiting. He was late. I saw a guy who fit the description and I approached, saying "Jim?" He said "yes" and we shook hands. After some small talk he looked confused and he said, "I'm Jim *Calabro*," and I realized I had the wrong guy so I apologized and we went our separate ways. But...I recognized his name as a writer who had just made a spec sale in *Variety*!

My guy never showed (mental note: never call *him* back), so I went home, determined to salvage this day of networking, and I looked up Jim Calabro's manager, a rep who had made several sales. I called the manager's office and told his assistant, "I'm a screenwriter, I was talking to his client Jim Calabro outside Urth Caffe and I wanted to tell him about my spec." She put me on hold and within 15 seconds I was pitching my script to the manager! I never would have got him on the phone if I was just another screenwriter making a cold call.

I had legitimized myself by dropping the right name with the right set of circumstances. I'd like to point out that, technically, I wasn't lying. He never asked for details and I didn't offer them. I got into my pitch as soon as I could.

Ultimately, he read my script and he passed. I didn't get signed, but I got my script in the door, which is the first directive of the aspiring screenwriter. You can't establish a career if you don't get your script read by the people that matter: the <u>decision-makers</u>.

There are some other key take-aways here:

- You need to be where the action is, most notably, Los Angeles, but another big city with a thriving film community can also work (New York, Austin, Vancouver, London, etc.).

- You need to have chutzpah (guts). Conquer your fear and pick up the phone.

- At the end of the day, there are no rules.

- Don't lie, but be prepared to get "creative" when necessary.

XVIII. GO TO MARKET, LITTLE PIGGY

As I've said, my motto is "Craft = Career," which means that the first and most important thing to establish your career is that you develop your writing skill and produce a great screenplay.

But that's not the *only* thing that will get your foot in the door. There are two sides to your career: there's your <u>work</u> and the <u>marketing</u> of your work. Marketing is a big commitment and challenge on its own. It's especially tough to muster the energy, discipline and perseverance to market your screenplay after you've spent months (or years) writing and polishing this opus! So you need to be in it for the long haul.

But before we get to marketing specifics, it's time to get tough. I have a serious question to ask you:

XIX. ARE YOU A *REAL* WRITER?

This is not a silly or obvious question. I've read too many scripts by writers who just don't have the basic writing skills to make a story work on the page or the discipline to put in the years of work it takes to develop a professional level of craft.

You don't have to *like* the actual process of writing – I've read countless interviews with professional writers who say they hate writing! They love *to have written*, to hold that completed draft in their hand, but the actual typing of the pages – the <u>work</u> – is like pulling teeth.

I would amend that to say that I think you don't need to enjoy the writing all the time, but you must enjoy it *some* of the time. For me, and many other writers, it's very difficult to actually sit down in front of the computer and type script pages. Procrastination is a huge temptation. Why does it always seem like the best time to clean the house is when I have to write? Why do I just happen to come up with my most brilliant Facebook statuses when I'm on deadline?

It can be torture to sit down and start writing, but once I really get in the zone – completely focused on the writing such that time has seemed to stop and I'm completely *in the story* – then I'm in heaven. I love being in that head space, in fact, I *need* to do it to relieve stress and be happy, but it's a pisser to get up the confidence and comfort level to begin.

But that's the gig. You have to be able to *do it*. Dedicate the time to sit down and bang out pages. Spend hours editing, tweaking, polishing, proofing. Write many, many drafts. And then when you're done with that script...do it all over again. Start a new one, and write that one faster and better.

If you can't commit to writing at least two spec scripts per year for the next three to four years, then you're not a real writer.

If you can only write with a partner or in ideal circumstances, you're not a real writer.

If you can't write in your time off from your full-time job, and that means nights and lunch breaks and weekends, then you're not a real writer.

The excuse "I can only write when I've shut out the world" is just that: an <u>excuse</u>. If you can only write on retreat in a log-cabin, then I only hope you have a wealthy benefactor, or you have a butt-load of vacation time saved up.

It takes discipline, an eye for detail, a dedication to excellence and a talent for written communication to be a real writer. You need to be able to spell and write grammatically correct sentences. It may sound like I'm pointing out the obvious, but you'd be surprised how many scripts I've read where the writer just didn't have the basic writing skills to tackle this form.

It starts with your high school English courses – did you get A's and B's in English or did you struggle just to get a C+? This may be a good barometer for you to assess your writing acumen. (Let's just say I'm hoping it was A's and B's.)

Have you ever been singled out by a teacher for writing an excellent essay, term paper or short story? I hope so.

Do you struggle with the proper usage of your, you're, there, they're, their, lose and loose? I *really* hope not (unless you have a Teflon-coated laptop).

Do you see yourself writing many scripts or just this one? If the answer is just one, then I can assure you that the time and effort it will take to create a great screenplay that has the potential to sell will far outstrip your commitment to the project. It's not worth it.

I'm sorry to say it, but too many of you just aren't writers. You may have a cool idea for a movie, or you're a cinephile or you're a gifted multi-media artist or a talented photographer. But that doesn't mean you're a good communicator *on the page*.

Output is a big part of the job. If you really, really struggle just to finish one draft, then you may not be a real writer. Not that it's *easy* to write a full draft; heck, it's tough to write 100 pages of anything. But if your biggest roadblock is completing a draft, then you're in trouble. The harsh truth is that you need to be able to do that if you're going to work as a professional writer.

You may know those writers that can bang out (sub-par) script after (sub-par) script or (unpublished) novel after (unpublished) novel. You may admire them for their output and wish you were so prolific. But the reason they can do this is because they don't have an internal editor. In other words, they're just cranking out pages without care about quality.

With that said, I must add, **no one has the right to tell you to stop writing.**

FROM THE TRENCHES:
AARON SORKIN
(The Social Network, A Few Good Men)

"**For years, I was working on an antiquated word processing program, which was fine for me but the writers' assistants would plead with me to let them install Final Draft on my computer. I'm a guy, I don't like change, so [I refused]. So they were brilliant, they simply lied to me. They told me my new computer 'is not compatible with your old software – it only recognizes Final Draft.'**"

The Lesson: Be open to change, not just with technology but with trends, working methods and collaborators.

FROM THE TRENCHES:

ICE-T
(New Jack City, Law & Order: SVU)

When I was a teenager, I saw Ice-T at a music festival greeting fans. I went up to him and I asked "Hey Ice, do you have any advice for a young filmmaker?" Without missing a beat, he said **"Yeah! TRY, TRY, DON'T STOP, TRY, TRY, DON'T STOP, TRY, DON'T STOP, DON'T STOP!"**

Great advice. I never forgot it. And here I am, just a few (cough) years older than a teenager and still trying.

I believe that if you enjoy it, you should do it. There's no shame in being a hobbyist. But if you aspire to compete at the professional level you must know that it's a very difficult path you've chosen, and it will take a lot of discipline and perseverance. You have to be passionate about your craft and career to push past frustration and rejection.

It should also be noted that you can't judge your ability or career on your first script. Ninety-nine percent of writers do not sell their first screenplay. But 100% of writers learn a tremendous amount about the form and format of screenwriting when they complete their first script. Once you're done with the first draft of your first script, I encourage you to analyze, edit, and rewrite it to get experience with the rewriting process. I also don't have a problem with paying a consultant to evaluate your first script as they can help you to locate your major issues of concern, and they will no doubt take months and maybe years off your development as a screenwriter. But you should still consider yourself in the learning stage.

So, with all that said, if you're still reading and still consider yourself a real writer (what hubris hath ye!), then here are some thoughts on marketing. Keep in mind these are just suggestions, not legal advice; I'm not a lawyer, manager or agent, so use it however you will.

XX. GETTING OUT THERE

Networking — The unfortunate truth about networking is that you need to give them something to get something. If you go in just asking for help from an industry professional, you will have the whiff of desperation that will turn them off. You want to set up a trade, rather than a charity case.

An assistant, development exec, producer, agent or manager is not going to waste time with you, and in most cases, not even take your call, unless you have something they want — a bit of information, a referral from a mutual friend, some air of "hotness," a fantastic logline or an undeniable Big Idea. The latter two are always a tough sell, though, because everyone reads a logline differently — what looks to be a definite home run with a brilliant hook to you might look stilted and cliché to them. You should go in knowing that it's going to be a fight to get people to read your material and to "get it" and see the potential in it to become a commercial movie.

The myth that everyone in Hollywood is constantly on the lookout for great material and thus is open to submissions from new screenwriters is one that screenwriters love to believe in, but in most cases, it is just that: a fantasy. This is supported by the myth that the current Hollywood system is broken, that the industry can't function without new blood and is on the verge of collapse as their budgets continue to go up and attendance goes down. I see this all the time on Internet message boards: some armchair box-office guru predicting that the studio system will crumble because they're not investing in new material, but rather investing in remakes, reboots and adaptations.

The studios are doing just fine. They wouldn't make these movies if they didn't turn a profit. They're making <u>billions</u>.

They have a system in place for script development. If they need a script, they don't post a query on Craigslist—they pick up the phone and call the twenty agents they have on speed-dial and ask for scripts—and they have at least twenty specs in their in-box by end of day.

With that said, why do they need *your* script, considering you're an un-sold, un-repped writer from the hinterlands?

The answer is: they don't.

It's your job to convince them that they do. It's your job to find the one decision-maker who will not only listen but will truly *feel* your pitch.

It's not easy, but it can be done. Cold calling can work. Networking <u>must</u> be done.

So how do you network with industry pros who won't take your call?

STATUS

If you're starting from scratch, not knowing anyone in the industry, then start with contacts at your same status: your fellow screenwriters. Start a writer's group in your hometown, join groups and message boards online and swap material. Again, you need to give something to get something. You can't sit back, be passive, and expect people to help you. With fellow writers, the way to build relationships is to give them notes. They will return notes in kind. Keep swapping notes with more and more writers and you will find ones with similar interests, genres of choice, and goals. If you come across a lazy, undisciplined, or poor writer, then move on to the next one.

Attend festivals and conferences, enter contests, post on message boards, hang out in creative centers and soon you'll have a network of hard-working up-and-coming screenwriters with which to share information, contacts, notes and support. From there, work your way up in status.

The next tier of status will be the assistants to the decision-makers.

Always be nice to the assistant and sell them on your script first, so that they will let you in the door with their boss. They are the gatekeeper to the big guy or gal. The assistant is looking to advance their career by finding good material, so they should have a vested interest in finding new writers; but it doesn't mean they will. They are overworked and underpaid and so they don't have the time or the energy to deal with every newbie writer that calls them up to pitch a logline. Since 9 out of 10 of these writers submit sub-par work, they've learned their lesson and so they will be more guarded when you call.

Timing is key. If you meet an exec at a conference, you need to follow up right away so that your opening line, "I met so-and-so at the Austin Conference and I was talking to her about my modern Western spec," is effective because the exec still remembers you. And if their assistant asks to take a message, then you need to be persistent and keep calling back.

My first boss after film school told me a story about a friend of his who kept calling Jodie Foster's office and leaving messages with her assistant. He was never put through. He kept calling, every day, over 50 times. One day, he got a call from Jodie Foster who said, simply, "Who are you and what do you want?"

I don't know what happened after that but, hey, at least he got Jodie Foster on the phone!

I'm not telling you to become a stalker. I'm just stressing that you need to be dogged in your determination. In fact, I suggest you follow this Cardinal Rule...

KILL 'EM WITH KINDNESS (AND STROKE THEIR EGO)

Whenever I make a phone call or write an email or query letter, I always thank them profusely and compliment them on their work. I mention how it would be an honor to get their insight on my work. I use words like "expertise" and "professional." I like to compliment them on their most recent success/ most successful box-office hit *and* one of their more obscure, critically-admired titles. They will be proud of that little indie they made, even if it tanked at the box-office, and they will love to hear from a fan, especially one who notices a detail about it that shows the level of craft that went into the making of this fine film.

Remember, every development professional not only wants to produce a box-office hit but they also have their passion projects that they hope to make someday to validate their vision and artistic sensibilities (and maybe pick up an Oscar or two, the ultimate ego stroke). If you treat them like a filmmaker that only makes *quality* films and tells *important* stories, they will love to hear it. Most of them, not all, are serious movie fans who follow their favorite directors and do actually want to make a classic film someday, not just *G.I. Joe 3: The Revenge*.

I also suggest you mention films that are similar in tone, style, genre and/or target audience, and they don't have to be big hits, either. I've gotten a lot of mileage out of comparing my supernatural thriller to *Donnie Darko*, even though *Darko* is a low-budget cult hit. There are many fans of *Darko* out there, so when they see the opportunity to tell a similar story, they are intrigued. In fact, I'd suggest you avoid comparisons to the monster blockbusters because no one is going to invest $200 million in your script anyway because you are an unproduced newbie with no talent attachments. You may have a superhero or fantasy script, but there's no comparison to *The Dark Knight* or *Harry Potter* as those films are massively budgeted with huge built-in audiences, so don't bother to mention them as you'll sound like an amateur.

And never, ever predict box-office performance, e.g., "This film is sure to gross at least $150 million and spawn two sequels. In fact, I have outlines for sequels already, which I can email you at any time, just ask!" These people sound like nutcases. This brings up a good point:

You're not an expert at the business of movie-making.

If anyone is, <u>they</u> are. So don't tell them how to do their job, and stick to your job: the writer. If they truly need you, then they want to know that you are a professional, dedicated, hard-working writer who comes up with great ideas and turns them into great screenplays. That's what they need you for, not to analyze last weekend's box-office returns, predict the financial future of the business or opine about digital distribution. They also want to know that you're a genial, social person who can carry a conversation, so if you come across as an impatient and critical know-it-all, then they will avoid you.

Do not say anything negative or criticize current movies. Do not say how comedies today are not funny and your script will finally make audiences laugh again (I've seen this done many times). For all you angry writers out there who think it's your calling to restore greatness to a genre that is obviously not up to the heights of yesteryear, you should look at the box-office to see how much *other people* are enjoying the current movies in that genre.

DO YOUR RESEARCH

The more you network and read the trades, the easier it will be to talk in "industry-speak" so you sound like you know what you're doing (even if you don't). You want to find out those current, specific terms and examples that folks in town are using in their discussions. For example, there's usually a few hot "subgenres," specific ways of classifying movies, which everyone's buzzing about.

Here are three sample subgenres -- can you name a hit movie from each one from the past 3 years?

- Elevated horror

- Home invasion horror

- Found footage horror

You must keep up on what's in theaters, what's hot at the box-office and what's in development so you can talk shop with that power player (and the underling that brings them their macchiato). You don't want to be one of those writers who only references movies from the seventies because "movies were just better back then." Yes, those writers may be working, but chances are, it's at a Starbucks near you.

XXI. INDIE VS. STUDIO

An important decision you want to make is whether you're writing a screenplay to break into the studio level of wide-release, commercial movies, or you're writing more for the independent or "art-house" film market.

FROM THE TRENCHES:

ROBERT ZEMECKIS
(Forrest Gump, Cast Away, Back To The Future)

"Enter the industry at the level you want to work."

A great option today is to produce your own low-budget, or "no-budget" feature film with high-resolution digital equipment. If this is your route, it may be a little bit less important to impress the reader with your screenplay than it would be if you were submitting to a major agency or studio; but consider that you're still going to be showing your script to many professionals that will be judging your ability to tell a cohesive and powerful story on the page; these readers will include investors, experienced crew members and professional actors and directors. So, unless you're developing your story from improvisations with a dedicated troupe of actors, you're still going to need a solid script.

If I had to point to one element that separates studio films from independent films, it would no longer be the use of an anti-hero, it would be the dark or ambiguous ending.

In *The Wrestler*, we don't know if Randy survives the big match or dies in the ring. *Sideways* ends with Miles knocking on Maya's door – there is hope but we don't actually <u>see</u>

them embrace. Can you imagine Kate Hudson *not* kissing the guy at the end of one of her many Rom-Coms?

Black Swan ends with Nina's death. You get the idea.

Since more studio films are dark these days, some indie films distinguish themselves by being *really* dark. In *Before the Devil Knows You're Dead*, all of the main characters are despicable. The younger brother (Ethan Hawke) is sleeping with his older brother's wife, while the older brother (Phillip Seymour Hoffman) is having an affair with a transvestite hooker, whom he later kills. Oh, and the main plot? The brothers mastermind a robbery of their own parents' jewelry store, which gets botched when their mother is shot! Even though it features major stars and was helmed by a legendary director (Sidney Lumet), this is a film that only could have been made and released outside the studio system.

If you're going the indie route, my advice is to end on what is most true to your story. Since you're writing for the reader, not for the VP of Marketing, you will impress them with the most "shocking yet inevitable" ending possible. One film that disappointed me with its ending is the powerful Cold War drama *The Lives of Others*. There is a crushing moment when the woman dies in the arms of her lover in the street. This should have been the Fade Out moment, showing the true devastation that the fascist regime brought to East Germany. But they tacked on a feel-good epilogue that, to me, felt extraneous and like an attempt at making it more commercial.

Remember not to be afraid to Get Extreme! And, as always...be elegant.

Or don't. Because that's the true indie way! Be an unabashed rebel and don't apologize for it.

Which reminds me of that question that is asked every day by budding filmmakers who cringe at the type of guidelines that I have put forth in this book. You know the one...

But what about Quentin Tarantino?

The answer is simple: You're not Quentin Tarantino.

XXII. YOUR FIRST SCREENPLAY

There's conventional wisdom you should follow, but which can be broken if you deliver a great script. But be prepared to accept that your first attempt is not going to be that great.

Most writers do not sell their very first screenplay. It acts as a <u>learning tool</u>.

I still suggest that you show your first script to others and that you rewrite it a couple times because you will learn a lot from this process, but I don't think you should go into it expecting for it to be your breakthrough script that will get you an option, a rep, some meetings or a sale. It is your crash course into the craft and the discipline.

Writers <u>write</u>. They don't just write one script. They *keep writing*. Not just to advance a career, but because they love it and there's an annoying little voice inside them that won't stop whispering. They have to write.

If you are a serious writer, then you are in it for the long haul.

The media loves to hail the "first time writer" who just made the big sale, but there's no way that a writer who sells a script didn't spend years learning and practicing their craft. Unless, perhaps, they are related to a big shot in the industry. There's a lot of nepotism in this business, but there's also limitless opportunities for new voices because this truly is a business with no hard and fast rules.

I recently read a review wherein the critic referred to the screenwriter as a "first-time writer." The truth is that this was the writer's first time as a *produced feature film writer*, but he had worked as a television writer for years (and probably optioned a few feature specs, as well). Everyone needs to ply their trade.

There are accepted guidelines and practices, and even though there are plenty of examples of these being broken, I still suggest you adhere to them. The first thing you can do is study and learn to utilize the structure and methods detailed in this book.

As for your writing process and long-term plan, I suggest you target the goal of writing two specs a year and that you develop your craft and writing method so that, once you have your Full Story Map and scene list polished, you can write a first draft in two to three months or less. On your first pass, the old maxim holds true: Don't get it right, just WRITE IT. In other words, power through it until the end. Don't try to get it perfect as you write; you'll have plenty of time to hone it in later drafts. Writing is rewriting, as they say.

It's okay for your first script to be a personal, "low-concept" story that you feel you need to get off your chest. Eventually, once you're more comfortable with the craft, you're going to want to develop a script that's more focused on a Big Idea in a commercially proven genre so you can catch the eye of producers and reps. To help increase your odds, I'd suggest you avoid:

Large ensemble pieces with lots of characters. They're not only expensive to shoot, but they're difficult to structure and to read because you're asking the reader to remember a lot of names.

Huge budget movies. When a studio greenlights an event movie, they hire one of the top 25 proven box-office hit writers in town to write it; they don't just pick a Joe off the street. With that said, your big-budget script may contain an awesome concept that will make them salivate, so it's possible they might option or buy your script and hire some established pros to rewrite it. But...a great concept is a great concept, and should be able to fit into a $10 or $20 million movie as well as a $100 million movie, so I encourage you to limit the need for CGI, car chases and famous buildings blowing up. Why blow up the White House when you can blow up an outhouse? (I think William Goldman said that. I could be wrong.)

Period pieces. They're expensive to make, especially those war epics that you newbies like to write.

Long scripts! You should already know that I highly suggest you gun for 100-110 pages. Even so, many of you will make that beginner mistake of writing (and submitting!) over 130 pages. To make matters worse, you will use tiny margins and print on thick paper. I once had a screenwriting instructor who said you should cut one-third of your first draft, no questions asked, before you write your second draft. Follow his advice.

Impenetrable titles. "The Malfeasance of Abercrombie Yoshihiro" is not a good title. *Star Wars* is. (And the original title of George Lucas' screenplay was *The Adventures of Luke Starkiller.* Thank Yoda he took someone's advice and changed it.)

Don't write about the movie industry and do NOT make your protagonist a screenwriter! People who work in the industry don't want an outsider's fantasy take on how it runs. Besides, most movies about movies <u>bomb</u>.

CONCLUSION

I want you to know that I applaud your courage in tackling this challenging creative endeavor and I hope you find my methods and advice to be helpful to your craft. If you're interested in learning more about Story Maps, working with me, or you just want to say hi, please do not hesitate to shoot me an email via my website at www.actfourscreenplays.com (and ask about **special offers and discounts** for my book readers on my services, classes and publications).

I encourage you to study the Full Story Maps that follow and their source films and to map your own favorite movies. I guarantee that you will advance your understanding of this exciting craft.

In closing, I leave you with the words that I speak to every writer I meet.

Good Luck and Happy Writing!

Dan Calvisi

APPENDIX:

SAMPLE STORY MAPS

95% of Great Movies follow the Story Map.

I find it tremendously helpful to look at produced films and note their elements in a Story Map, creating a quick-reference "library" of maps to compare and contrast. This is the best way to understand how the pros do it.

I encourage you to story map all of your favorite movies.

Remember, the Story Map is a <u>form</u>, not a formula. It does not dictate your choices—it does not tell you what to write—it only provides a framework to hold your choices. The screenplay is still undeniably yours, but it now comes wrapped in the shiny coating that is recognized by every Agent, Manager, Executive and Producer in the business.

Below are maps for a wide range of films to use as reference tools. Once you've studied these, feel free to ask me about obtaining more maps of successful movies.

FULL STORY MAPS:

1. The Hangover (Comedy) 2009

2. The Wrestler (Drama) 2008

3. The Dark Knight (Action/Comic Book) 2008

4. How to Lose a Guy in 10 Days (Romantic Comedy) 2003

5. Drag Me To Hell (Horror) 2009

6. As Good As It Gets (Dramatic Comedy) 1998

7. Sunset Boulevard (Noir Thriller) 1950

Although we have three central characters in *The Hangover*, the "main" protagonist is Stu, played by Ed Helms, because he is the character who goes through the most change.

The script is a great example of a comedy that offers multiple set pieces with escalating conflict, lots of visual devices and clever setups and payoffs.

THE HANGOVER (2009)
Written by Jon Lucas & Scott Moore
Directed by Todd Phillips
Running Time: 98 mins.

BASIC STORY MAP

PROTAGONIST: STU, 30s, dentist

> **Misbehavior**: Constantly worried and always sees the worst
> **Skill**: Nice guy
> **Flaw/Achilles Heel**: He's a wimp

EXTERNAL GOAL: To find Doug

INTERNAL GOAL: To dump his awful girlfriend Melissa

MAIN DRAMATIC CONFLICT: Their memory loss and the previous night's antics

THEME: Loyalty and True Friendship

CENTRAL DRAMATIC QUESTION: Can the guys find Doug in time for the wedding and can Stu find love?

ENDING: Stu breaks up with Melissa and the guys look at photos from the weekend, vowing to delete them once they're done.

ARC: Stu goes from a wimpy victim to a take-charge guy with a promising romantic life.

LOGLINE
A group of friends with no memory of their sordid bachelor party must piece together the events of the night to find the missing groom before the wedding the next day.

FULL STORY MAP

STORY ENGINES

ACT 1: The guys go to Las Vegas and kick off the night with a toast.

ACT 2A: The guys follow their initial clues to find Doug.

ACT 2B: The guys must return Mike Tyson's tiger and bring Mr. Chao his money to get back Doug.

ACT 3: The wedding goes off well and Stu dumps Melissa.

THE BEAT SHEET
(note: this is not a complete scene list)

ACT ONE

1-2 — **OPENING** (FLASHFORWARD): Preparations on wedding day; the groom is missing. TRACY, the bride, gets a call from PHIL, who's in the Nevada desert, looks beaten up. Phil tells Tracy they lost Doug, the groom. The wedding is "not gonna happen."

Central Dramatic Question: Will they miss the wedding and how did they lose the groom?

3 – ALAN, the odd brother-in-law of DOUG, the groom, joins him for a tux fitting. Alan is concerned that Doug's friends don't like him.

5 – Alan tells Doug he will never tell anyone what happens in Vegas.

6 – Doug promises his future father-in-law (Jeffrey Tambor) that he's the only one that will drive his car.

6 – Meet Phil, junior high school teacher. He pockets the kids' field trip money for his Vegas fund.

7 – STU lies to his controlling bitch girlfriend MELISSA that the guys are going to Napa for a wine-tasting trip.

9-10 – **INCITING INCIDENT:** The guys start their journey by driving on the highway to Vegas. Alan almost gets them hit by a truck! The problems have already begun.

16 – They enter their huge suite (which Phil forced Stu to rent after reminding him that Melissa cheated on him with a bartender on a cruise).

17 – Stu shows them the ring he'll propose to Melissa with – it was his grandma's ring she kept since the holocaust. Phil warns Stu not to marry her.

18 – They guys leave the room to hit the town.

20 – **STRONG MOVEMENT FORWARD:** On the roof of the hotel, the guys toast with liquor from Alan.

23 – The next morning – the suite has been trashed. The guys wake up to find a chicken, a tiger, and Stu has a missing tooth. They <u>don't remember anything</u>.

27 – **END OF ACT ONE TURN (EXTERNAL):** Doug is missing! His cell phone has been left behind.

28 – **END OF ACT ONE TURN (INTERNAL):** There's a baby in the closet! (This will lead Stu to his love interest)

30 – **DECISION**: They start to gather clues to piece together the previous 12 hours and find Doug: receipts, a valet ticket, a hospital bracelet on Phil's wrist.

ACT TWO-A

32 – Doug's mattress was thrown out the window of the hotel.

32 – The valet brings their car – it's a police sedan!

34 – They talk to the Doctor at the hospital who treated Phil last night. Phil had Rufalin in his system, which explains the memory loss. They must have all been drugged.

38 – At the Best Little Chapel, they look at Stu's wedding photos to a woman who goes by the name "Jade."

41 – **FIRST TRIAL/FIRST CASUALTY:** Asian gangsters pull up and try to kill

them, asking "Where is he?" They assume they are also looking for Doug. The guys barely escape in the cop car.

42 – They find JADE, the stripper that Stu married. They give her back her baby. She doesn't know where Doug went.

45 – **COMBAT:** COPS storm in, arrest the guys!

50 – Cops use the guys as test subjects for tasers and stun guns in a class with kids. Stu gets shot in the neck, Phil in the nuts and Alan in the face.

53 – They locate the car, it looks fine. They're optimistic.

55 – **MIDPOINT:** A naked Asian guy jumps out of the trunk, hits them all with a crowbar and runs off! Alan admits he put a drug in their drinks last night. He thought it was Ecstasy but it turned out to be rufi's. They hit bottom.

ACT TWO-B

58 – Mike Tyson is in their hotel suite. He came to get his tiger. The guys must return it.

65-67 – Mike Tyson shows them their antics on his security cams; they know Doug was alive as of 3:30 am so they are once again optimistic.

70-72 – <u>CLOCK</u>: MR. CHAO, the formerly naked guy and the head of the Asian gang, gives them until dawn the next day to return the $80k of poker chips they stole from him or he will kill Doug, who is hooded and gagged in the backseat of his car!

74-76 – **DECLARATION OF WAR/ASSUMPTION OF POWER:** The "Rainman" blackjack sequence; Alan and crew work a table and win $82,000.

79 – They make trade with gangsters in desert, the money for the hostage, but he's not their Doug; it's Doug the drug dealer who sold Alan the pills.

81 – We catch up to the Opening Flash-Foward as Phil calls Tracy in desert.

83 – Alan figures it out, tackles Phil before he can tell Tracy they lost Doug.

84 – **TURN (External):** They find Doug on the roof of the hotel, sunburned but still alive!

85 – All the flights are booked, they need to drive back to make the wedding.

86 – **TURN (Internal):** Jade gives Stu his ring back. Stu asks her out on a date for next weekend.

88 – **DECISION:** They leave for L.A. Phil drives like a maniac. Doug tells them he found Mr. Chao's $80k in poker chips! They get a delivery of tuxes on the highway and change clothes on the side of the road.

90 – They pull up, get there just in time!

ACT THREE

91 – **TRUE PT. OF NO RETURN:** Just as they are to be married, Doug vows to never put Tracy through this again and she forgives him.

92 – Phil reunites with his wife and kid, showing he's a good guy, after all.

93 – **CLIMAX (INTERNAL):** Stu tells off Melissa in front of everyone and breaks up with her.

95 – **CLIMAX (EXTERNAL):** Alan found Stu's camera with pictures. They all agree to watch them once and then delete them, sealing their secret forever.

96 – **EPILOGUE:** Wild photo montage.

98 – <u>END</u>

The Wrestler is a great example of a focused, intimate character study set in a world that we'd never seen portrayed on film with such verisimilitude. An unflinching modern tragedy, the screenplay uses very little subtext but this style works perfectly in portraying a flamboyant protagonist who wears his heart, his machismo and his personal demons on his sleeve. There is nothing subtle about Randy "The Ram" Robinson and the script reflects that.

THE WRESTLER (2008)
Screenplay by Robert Siegel
Directed by Darren Aronofsky
Running Time: 105 mins.

BASIC STORY MAP

PROTAGONIST: Randy "The Ram" Robinson, 50's, washed-up wrestler.
   Misbehavior: His ego

   Skill: Wrestling

   Flaw/Achilles Heel: Addicted to fame

EXTERNAL GOAL: To reclaim his wrestling glory

INTERNAL GOAL: To win over Cassidy and reconcile with his daughter

MAIN DRAMATIC CONFLICT: Himself

THEME: Pride goeth before the fall.

CENTRAL DRAMATIC QUESTION: Will Randy give up wrestling for good and win the hearts of both his daughter and Cassidy?

ENDING: Randy rejects Cassidy for the glory of the wrestling ring.

ARC: Randy goes from a broken, washed-up wrestler to a man in search of love, but ultimately gives up hope for the glory of the wrestling ring.

LOGLINE

A washed-up pro wrestler pursues a rematch bout to win back his fame but it could cost him his girlfriend, his daughter and his life.

FULL STORY MAP

STORY ENGINES

Act 1: Randy struggles just to pay his rent by competing in brutal wrestling matches.

Act 2A: Randy suffers a heart attack and is forced to change his ways. He falls for a stripper (Cassidy) who encourages him to reconcile with his daughter.

Act 2B: Randy attempts to turn his life around but can't stop his destructive ways and he decides to wrestle in the big rematch with the Ayatollah.

Act 3: Randy rejects all for the glory of the wrestling ring, going to his certain death.

THE BEAT SHEET
(note: this is not a complete scene list)

ACT ONE

1 – OPENING IMAGES: A glory days collage of Randy "The Ram" Robinson's career over Quiet Riot's "Metal Health."

3 – **OPENING**: 20 years later...Randy's a washed-up wrestler, reduced to performing in small-town school gyms.

5 – **INCITING INCIDENT**: Randy arrives at his trailer to find it's locked: rent's not paid, so he must sleep in his van.

9 - At the grocery store, Randy asks his condescending boss for more hours.

13 – Wrestling match – Randy slices his forehead with a hidden razor blade for dramatic effect. Bloody, he wins the match.

17 – **STRONG MOVEMENT FORWARD (External)**: EMT cleans up Randy after match as the promoter pitches him on a rematch between Randy and the Ayatollah. Randy accepts.

20 – **STRONG MOVEMENT FORWARD (Internal)**: Randy defends his favorite stripper, Cassidy, from young men (they make fun of her age). Cassidy's

angry at first, but gives Randy a lap dance. She listens to his stories, gives affection, but there's a distance...after all, she's a stripper.

24 – Randy buys HGH from a pusher at the gym, injects and works out. Gets hair dyed, tans -- costly maintenance.

28 – END OF ACT ONE TURN: Randy's new wrestling match includes a dangerous escalation: barbed wire, broken glass and a staple gun.

29 – DECISION: Randy competes even though he's obviously being hurt.

ACT TWO-A

35-36 FIRST TRIAL/FIRST CASUALTY: Randy suffers a heart attack and wakes up in a hospital. Doctor instructs him to stop using drugs and, most importantly, give up wrestling: he could die.

40 – Randy pays his rent and his landlord unlocks the trailer.

45 – COMBAT: Randy asks Cassidy out. She says no, but she talks to him and encourages him to see his daughter.

50 – Randy finds his daughter, Stephanie. He tells her about his heart attack and she rejects him.

56 – Randy asks the boss for more work; gets a job at the deli counter.

58 – Cassidy allows Randy to call her by her real name (Pam) and helps him pick out a coat for his daughter. After he asks her out for a beer, she tells him she has a child and Randy gives her a gift: a Randy The Ram action figure.

60 – MIDPOINT: Randy kisses Cassidy (This directly pushes to the climax where Randy must choose between wrestling fame and love).

ACT TWO-B

63 – Randy works his new job at the deli counter and his name-tag reads "Robin" -- his birth-name (he's decided to be himself, not play a role).

68-72 – Randy cancels his upcoming matches; officially retires. Randy apologizes to Stephanie for leaving her.

75 – **ASSUMPTION OF POWER**: Randy dances with his daughter. He asks her out to dinner and she accepts.

77 – Randy goes to strip club and gives Cassidy a thank you card. He wants a relationship, but Cassidy, unable to separate him from a customer, rejects the idea. Randy gets upset, offends her and leaves.

80-83 – Randy parties with his fellow wrestlers, does coke and has sex with a girl at a bar. He misses the date with his daughter.

85 – **END OF ACT TWO TURN**: Randy goes to Stephanie's house and she kicks him out of her life for good -- she can't deal with the pain.

89-90 – **DECISION**: Randy quits his supermarket job, calls the promoter and agrees to do the Ayatollah rematch.

ACT THREE

91 – Montage of Randy getting ready for the rematch.

93 – Cassidy breaks up with Randy. Randy acts like it doesn't faze him and invites her to the Ayatollah rematch.

95 – Cassidy quits the strip club.

97 – **TRUE POINT OF NO RETURN**: Randy chooses the crowd over Cassidy: "You hear them? This is where I belong."

103-105 – **CLIMAX:** Randy feels pain in his chest, but continues. The Ayatollah recognizes it and goes down, but Randy won't pin him. The crowd chants "Ram Jam," Randy looks to the wings and finds Cassidy gone. Randy climbs on the ropes...leaps...and we CUT TO BLACK.

The Dark Knight is an expert example of building an active story around Theme and pushing the story to the extremes of the conflict. At 144 minutes, this is a long, complex story, so I've adjusted the page placements in the latter half of the map.

THE DARK KNIGHT (2008)
Screenplay by Jonathan Nolan and Christopher Nolan
Story by Christopher Nolan & David S. Goyer
Directed by Christopher Nolan
Running Time: 144 minutes

BASIC STORY MAP

PROTAGONIST: BRUCE WAYNE/ BATMAN, 30s, crime fighter and billionaire

> **Skill:** Physical strength and incredible technology

> **Misbehavior:** Stubbornness; pure loner, will not accept help or advice

> **Achilles Heel:** His love for Rachel

EXTERNAL GOAL: To save Gotham City from destruction

INTERNAL GOAL: To be with Rachel / To preserve the hope of Gotham's people

MAIN DRAMATIC CONFLICT: The Joker

THEME: Desperation and fear lead to destructive actions.

CENTRAL DRAMATIC QUESTION: Can Bruce Wayne retire Batman and let Harvey Dent clean up Gotham?

ENDING: Bruce Wayne decides to let Batman take the fall for Harvey Dent's murders to maintain Dent as a hero and save Gotham City.

ARC: Bruce Wayne goes from believing he can end all crime in Gotham City as its hero to sacrificing Batman's good name to save Gotham City from destruction.

LOGLINE

Bruce Wayne struggles to position Harvey Dent as Gotham's white knight as the Joker reigns terror on the city, forcing Bruce to either reveal his identity or to kill The Joker to preserve the peace in Gotham City.

FULL STORY MAP

STORY ENGINES

ACT 1: Bruce fights organized crime in Gotham City with the aid of District Attorney Harvey Dent.

ACT 2A: Bruce puts away the mob, but must fight the new, more deadly threat: The Joker. Bruce decides to turn himself in to protect innocent lives.

ACT 2B: Bruce's use of force cannot stop the Joker, leading to Rachel's death and Harvey Dent becoming Two-Face.

ACT 3: Bruce must stop The Joker and Two-Face and make a final sacrifice to preserve hope in the people of Gotham.

THE BEAT SHEET
(note: this is not a complete scene list)

ACT ONE

1-5 – Opening sequence: a team of masked crooks robs a mob-owned bank. A suicidal move. The "silent Robber" kills off the last member of the bank heist crew.

6 – The silent Robber removes his mask: he is THE JOKER. He brilliantly escapes in broad daylight with all of the money.

10 – INCITING INCIDENT, EXTERNAL "A" story (Batman saving Gotham City): Batman catches The Scarecrow and key members of Maroni's mob.

11 – INCITING INCIDENT, EXTERNAL "B" story (Batman vs. Joker): Batman pledges to Police Lieutenant JIM GORDON that he will stop The Joker.

13 – INCITING INCIDENT, INTERNAL (Rachel, love story): RACHEL is dating HARVEY DENT, the new District Attorney. Bruce is jealous.

13 – Alfred tries to get Bruce to accept his limits. Bruce replies "Batman has no limits." (Subtheme of Identity: Can Bruce live without Batman?)

18 – LUCIUS FOX, CEO of Wayne Enterprises (and Batman's tech genius) considers a business deal with MR. LAO, a possibly corrupt Chinese businessman.

20 – STRONG MOVEMENT FORWARD, "A" story: Bruce crashes Rachel and Harvey's date. Bruce is convinced Harvey is legit, offers to throw him a fundraiser.
> ***Key dialogue:*** Harvey: "You either die a hero or live to become the villain."

22 – Lao is working with Maroni's mob crew; he has moved all their money to Hong Kong, where he currently sits, protected from extradition.

23 - 25 – The Joker crashes the mob meeting, tells them he's their only chance at killing Batman. In exchange for him killing Batman, he wants half of all their money. They put a bounty on his head.

27 – END OF ACT ONE TURN: Batman offers to bring Lao back from Hong Kong so Dent can prosecute Lao and Maroni's crew.

28 – DECISION: Bruce begins his plot to get Lao.

30 – Joker kills Gamble and starts to take over the mob.

ACT TWO-A:

38 – FIRST TRIAL: Bruce extricates Lao and drops him off at the Gotham police station. Rachel interrogates him; she and Dent come up with a plan to prosecute the entire mob.

40 – Gordon arrests Maroni's entire crew. They are all prosecuted by Dent.

42 – FIRST CASUALTY: The Joker's first public murder: he has killed the copycat Batman vigilante (seen earlier); The Joker releases a chilling video clip to the media.

43 – Joker's threat: Batman must reveal his identity or Joker will kill more people. Bruce dismisses the notion.

45 – COMBAT (Internal): Bruce's penthouse fundraiser for Dent: "I believe in Harvey Dent." Bruce tells Rachel that he will retire as Batman since Harvey Dent is Gotham's true hero. She feels pressured.

47 – Gordon and his cops figure out that The Joker is targeting three victims: Police Commissioner Loeb, the Judge and Harvey Dent.

48-49 – Harvey asks Rachel to marry him. She doesn't have an answer yet. Judge and Police Commissioner assassinated. Joker shows up at fundraiser.

52 – COMBAT (External): Batman fights Joker and his henchman. Joker throws Rachel out window. Batman saves her.

56 – Joker's next target: Mayor Garcia.

59 – Bruce's technology finds a clue and he speeds to the funeral parade site on his motorcycle.

62 – Joker attempts to shoot Mayor, hits Gordon, KILLING HIM.

67 – Dent goes over the line and tortures the henchman. Batman stops him. Bruce <u>decides to give up his identity</u>, tells Harvey to hold a press conference. Harvey objects.

69 – Rachel tells Bruce not to give in, but she will be with him if he goes legit; they kiss.

70 – Bruce has Alfred burn all of Batman's records. Alfred tells him not to give up his identity, but he respects Bruce's decision.

72 – MIDPOINT: Bruce is about to give himself in when Harvey steps in, says he's Batman. Harvey is arrested.

73 – MIDPOINT (Internal): Rachel gives Alfred a letter for Bruce for "when the time is right."

ACT TWO-B:

76 – Joker attacks convoy with Harvey Dent inside.

78 – Batman saves Harvey and chases The Joker on the BATPOD, his new motorcycle that ejects from the Tumbler.

83 – Batman refuses to kill Joker, skids out. Gordon, ALIVE, catches The Joker.

88 – DECLARATION OF WAR/ASSUMPTION OF POWER: Batman loses control and begins to torture Joker by beating him. It doesn't work. Joker tells him that the people of Gotham will turn on themselves.

89 [Standard length Turn*] – Joker has Dent and Rachel. Batman must choose whom to save.

90 [Standard length Decision*] – Batman chooses to save Rachel; Gordon rushes to save Dent.

Note: although this Act Two is longer than a "standard-length" feature film and will not end until minute/page 106, it's interesting to note that there is still a Turn and Decision in the exact same range as in a standard-length feature film, which is done to adhere to the audience's expectations of traditional pacing/structure.

96 – <u>Rachel is killed</u>. Dent's face is burned. The Joker escapes from jail with Lau.

97 – Batman at the ashes. Alfred reads Rachel's letter: she said she was marrying Harvey Dent.
   Key Dialogue: Rachel V.O.: "I believe the day will come when Gotham no longer needs Batman, but I don't think the day will come when Bruce Wayne doesn't need Batman."

98 – Bruce believes that Rachel was going to wait for him. Alfred refrains from giving him the letter.

100 – Dent wakes up in hospital, goes mad. His coin has become scuffed on one side.

103 – The Joker burns his money, completes his take-over of the mob and readies his final assault on Gotham.

104 – **END OF ACT TWO TURN:** Joker calls in to the TV show with an ultimatum: kill Reese (guy blackmailing Bruce Wayne) in 60 minutes or Joker will blow up a hospital.

105 – **DECISION:** Bruce goes into action to protect Reese.

ACT THREE:

107-112 – Joker has infiltrated the hospital in disguise, visits Harvey and begins to recruit him. Harvey becomes Two-Face. Bruce saves Reese. Joker blows up Gotham General hospital, escapes once again.

113 – Joker's threat: get out by nightfall or the city will burn.

117 – **TRUE POINT OF NO RETURN** – Lucius tells Batman the sonar is wrong; "This is too much power for one man. Spying on 30 million people is not part of my job description." Lucius will help him one more time, then resign. Bruce accepts his resignation.

119 – Prisoners and civilians are being evacuated on separate ferries.

120 – Ferries taken over by Joker's plan; rigged to explode. Joker has given each boat the detonator for the other boat.

122 – The two boats start to fight over detonating the bombs.

124 – Batman ignores Gordon's orders and charges into Joker's location to take out his men and save the civilian hostages they are holding.

129 – Batman finds Joker. Joker gets upper hand, beating him with a lead pipe.

130 – On both boats, a man volunteers to detonate the other boat.

132 – Joker holds Batman at bay, promises him the boats will explode when one person pushes the button. They don't; the Joker's test of human nature in the face of fear has failed.

133 – Batman apprehends The Joker. The Joker monologues, comparing himself to Bruce, how they are both freaks, misunderstood by normal society (subtheme of Identity). He reveals that Harvey Dent/Two-Face is his back-up plan -- Harvey's corruption will destroy the hope of Gotham's citizens.

139 – Batman saves Gordon's family from Two-Face. Two-Face killed.

142 – **CLIMAX (EXTERNAL AND INTERNAL)**: Bruce decides to take the fall for Harvey's killing spree. Dent will remain Gotham's hero and Batman its outlaw. Batman will let himself be hunted, once again a criminal, SAVING GOTHAM CITY FROM DESTRUCTION.

143 - 144 – **EPILOGUE:** Gordon tells media about Harvey Dent being Gotham's knight, but we know he's really talking about Batman. Alfred burns the letter from Rachel. Lucius Fox resigns, destroys the sonar spy system. Batman runs from police.

How to Lose a Guy in 10 Days quickly develops a simple, clean throughline built on two characters with opposing goals—she must scare him off and he must get her to fall in love with him—then uses clever set pieces to escalate conflict along the way.

HOW TO LOSE A GUY IN 10 DAYS (2003)

Screenplay by Kristen Buckley & Brian Regan and Burr Steers
based on the book by Michele Alexander and Jeannie Long
Directed by Donald Petrie
Running Time: 110 mins.

BASIC STORY MAP

PROTAGONIST: ANDIE ANDERSON, 20s, magazine writer

> **Misbehavior:** Competitive
>
> **Skill:** Playing the "psycho girlfriend"
>
> **Flaw/Achilles Heel:** Likes Ben's family

EXTERNAL GOAL: To get Ben to dump her in 10 days

INTERNAL GOAL: To fall in love with Ben/To be a serious writer

MAIN DRAMATIC CONFLICT: BEN

THEME: Being truthful with your partner and yourself

CENTRAL DRAMATIC QUESTION: Can Andie scare away Ben in 10 days or will she fall for him?

ENDING: Andie and Ben get together.

ARC: Andie goes from a cynical ambition to finding her soul mate.

LOGLINE

A magazine columnist must get a guy to dump her in 10 days to meet a deadline while he must get her to fall in love with him to win a lucrative ad account.

FULL STORY MAP

STORY ENGINES

ACT 1: Andie must date a guy and scare him off while Ben must make a woman fall for him. They meet and start their schemes, both in denial that there is a spark.

ACT 2A: Andie does her best to make Ben run away, but he will not dump her.

ACT 2B: Andie falls for Ben after meeting his family and she tries to get out of writing the article but she's stuck.

ACT 3: Andie and Ben find out the truth about their respective motivations and have a big public fight. Andie writes the article as an apology and Ben rushes after her and they make up.

THE BEAT SHEET
(note: this is not a complete scene list)

ACT ONE

1 – **OPENING**: ANDIE ANDERSON is the "How To" girl at Composure Magazine. She writes about situations that she lives, but what she REALLY wants to do is write serious pieces like her story about bringing peace to Tajikhistan. But this is not right for a fluffy women's magazine. Andie has two female coworkers who are her ALLIES.

5 – BEN needs to win the diamond account at his ad agency. He and his two ALLIES, his co-worker buddies, must beat out the two Judy's, who currently have his boss's eye.

10 – **INCITING INCIDENT**: Andie's boss LANA shoots down her proposal to write serious columns. Andie must write an article about what NOT to do with guys. Lana dubs it "How to Lose a Guy in 10 Days." 10 days is Andie's deadline to go to press. She must find a guy fast and start dating him as the girlfriend from hell, or she'll never win Lana's approval to write serious articles.

12 – The Judy's meet Andie and hear about her quest to drop a guy in 10 days.

17 – **STRONG MOVEMENT FORWARD:** Ben must make a woman fall in love with him and take this woman to the big diamond party...in 10 days. Judy sees Andie in the bar and chooses her, knowing she's a lost cause for Ben.

20 – Ben picks up Andie -- both are enthusiastic to meet one another, for their own secret and opposing reasons.

First Date – Andie tries to scare Ben and he's trying to be romantic and listen.

27 – **END OF ACT ONE TURN:** They KISS, and for a moment it seems like both forget about their schemes. As the night ends, both think they have the upper hand.

29 – **DECISION**: Andie's scheme with the Knicks tickets works. Ben thinks it's his scheme.

ACT TWO-A

31 – Their second date, the Knicks game; Andie ruins the game for Ben.

39 -40 – **FIRST STRIKE/FIRST CASUALTY:** Andie takes him to a chick flick, where Ben gets punched out. As Andie cradles him, there's a SPARK there; she likes him. Her plan is in jeopardy.

55 – **MIDPOINT:** Andie shows Ben her Family Album: pics of their future children she made with Photoshop. Ben's mother calls Andie at his apartment, Andie bonds with her. New throughline: Andie joining Ben's family.

60 – **WAR:** Andie crashes Ben's poker party. He explodes and breaks up with her, but his allies convince him to patch it up or they'll lose the ad account. He suggests couples therapy.

ACT TWO-B

75 – DECLARATION OF WAR/ASSUMPTION OF POWER: The "Bullshit" card game -- Andie fails at first but starts to beat Ben with the help of his family. Family tells her she was the first person to beat Ben, and the first girl he ever brought home.

80 – Andie expresses real feelings for Ben. His mom "really hugged" her, she was touched.

82 – Andie and Ben make love. She has completely fallen for him.

86 – END OF ACT TWO TURN: Andie tries to get out of the article, but Lana won't let her off the hook. She has two days to finish it by deadline. She's stuck.

87 – DECISION: Andie decides to go ahead with the article.

ACT THREE

92 – At the diamond party, Ben's Boss gives him and his allies the diamond account.

94 – Guys tell Andie about Ben's bet and Lana tells Ben about Andie's article. They both know the truth.

95 – Andie causes a scene on stage, calls Ben up for a song. Both fight in song.

100 – TRUE POINT OF NO RETURN: They break up. Andie lost Ben and broke her heart.

102 – Andie quits her job when her boss won't let her write about politics.

105 – Ben is given Andie's article by his Ally; Andie wrote that she made the biggest mistake of her life. (note: Andie's climactic action is to write this article, but this action is largely offscreen, which is a flaw in the film, IMHO.)

106 – Ben realizes he loves her – he must catch her before she leaves for Wash, D.C. for a new job. Ben chases after her cab on his motorcycle.

108 – **CLIMAX:** Ben catches Andie on the Brooklyn Bridge. She thinks she's doing the right thing and it's the only way she can be a true writer – he calls "Bullshit!" He knows she's only running away. They kiss.

110 – END.

On the job as a reader, one of the most glowing coverage reports I ever gave was to Sam and Ivan Raimi's "The Curse." It was a perfect fit for my employer at the time, but for reasons unknown to me, the script didn't get set up.

The film took years to get made and it was ultimately renamed "Drag Me To Hell." The result is a tight horror story that never stops moving forward with cleverly plotted set pieces and escalating conflict until a bold, BIG ENDING. Sure, there's a lot of disgusting goo and shameless shock cuts, but, you have to admit, it's a lot of fun, right?

Note how the length is short so the signpost beats after the Midpoint fall earlier than they would with a 110 page script.

DRAG ME TO HELL (2009)
Written by Sam Raimi & Ivan Raimi
Directed by Sam Raimi
Running Time: 93 mins.

BASIC STORY MAP

PROTAGONIST: CHRISTINE, 20's, farm girl turned loan officer
  Misbehavior: Passive

  Skill: Hidden strength (she's a fighter when pushed)

  Flaw/Achilles Heel: Dishonest

EXTERNAL GOAL: To escape the curse

INTERNAL GOAL: To get the promotion to Assistant Manager

MAIN DRAMATIC CONFLICT: Mrs. Ganush

THEME: Take responsibility for your actions

CENTRAL DRAMATIC QUESTION: How will Christine survive the curse?

ENDING: Christine makes a fatal mistake and is dragged into hell!

ARC: Christine goes from a meek girl who blames her treatment of Mrs. Ganush on her boss to a fighter who ultimately owns up to her mistake.

LOGLINE

A meek loan officer has three days to escape a gypsy curse that will damn her to hell.

FULL STORY MAP

STORY ENGINES

ACT 1: Christine tries to prove herself to her boss but she is cursed and attacked by Mrs. Ganush.

ACT 2A: Christine fights against the Lamia's attacks and struggles to rid herself of the curse.

ACT 2B: Christine fails to win over Clay's parents and the séance goes awry.

ACT 3: Christine must give the curse back to Mrs. Ganush but she makes an error, sealing her fate.

THE BEAT SHEET

(note: this is not a complete scene list)

ACT ONE

1-3 **OPENING:** Pasadena, 1969 – SHAUN SAN DENA, a young exorcist, fails to protect a little boy from the curse of the Lamia. He is dragged into hell and she vows, "We shall meet again."

3-5 Creepy title sequence with woodcuts, we see book of spells, images of possessions and demons. Rule: "3 days for the curse to develop."

6 – At the bank where she works, CHRISTINE congratulates a nice couple on a home loan. The Assistant Manager desk is empty.

7 – Her boss, MR. JACKS, tells her the Asst. Mgr. position is between her and STU, the new guy who's "able to make the tough choices."

8 – Christine visits CLAY DALTON, her boyfriend. She found him a 1929 "liberty" quarter for his coin collection; he puts it in a white envelope.

9 – Christine overhears Clay talking to his mother on the speaker phone; Mom doesn't like Christine, the "girl from the farm."

10 – **INCITING INCIDENT:** Gypsy woman, MRS. GANUSH, begs Christine to give her another extension on her mortgage so she doesn't lose her home.

13-16 – Christine rejects Mrs. Ganush, who begs on her knees, making a scene in the bank. Mr. Jacks tells Chrstine she's at the top of list for Asst. Manager.

18-21 – **STRONG MOVEMENT FORWARD:** In the dark parking garage, Mrs. Ganush ambushes Christine. They have a brutal fight and Christine shows hidden strength, but Mrs. Ganush pulls a button off her coat, curses it, saying "Lamia."

28 – **END OF ACT ONE TURN:** Rham Jas, psychic fortune teller, reads Christine's palm and tells her she was cursed. Clay tries to convince Christine that Rham is a con artist.

30 – **DECISION:** Christine trusts that Clay is right and stays at home alone that night with his kitten.

ACT TWO-A

33 – Christine is attacked by the ghost of the Lamia, knocked down, gets a split lip! She keeps it a secret from Clay so he doesn't think she's crazy.

40 – **FIRST TRIAL/FIRST CASUALTY:** At bank, Christine spews blood all over her boss and Stu steals her file for the big loan she's been working on.

41 – Christine visits home of Mrs. Ganush, which is filled with gypsy revelers. Christine tries to tell Ganush's niece that it was her boss' decision to throw out Mrs. Ganush, not hers.

44 – **COMBAT:** Christine doesn't realize it's a funeral—she backs into the coffin holding the dead Mrs. Ganush and the body falls on top of Christine— embalming fluid spills into Christine's mouth!

44 – Rham Jas explains she's been cursed by the Lamia, the black goat. The rules: after three days, the Lamia will come for the cursed button and take her to hell. Christine can't sacrifice an animal to ward off the curse as Rham suggests.

50 – **MIDPOINT:** After another attack from the Lamia, even worse this time, Christine kills Clay's kitten! Thinks the curse is lifted.

ACT TWO-B

52 – Christine meets Clay's wealthy parents; his MOTHER is a major bitch.

58 – Christine's hallucinations return; she coughs up a fly and freaks out. Clay's mother tells him not to go after her.

60 – **WAR (External):** Ram Jas tells Christine that her only hope is Shaun San Dena, but it will cost $10,000. She has <u>one day left</u> before the Lamia comes for her.

61 – **WAR (Internal):** Christine loses the assistant manager job to Stu because her deal fell through.

64 – Clay comes to her aid: he paid Ram Jas the money for the exorcism.

66 – Christine meets the older Shaun San Dena (from the opening flashback), ready to get her revenge on the Lamia.

68 – Set piece: the séance. Shaun San Dena explains the rules: she will make the Lamia possess her, Christine must put Dena's hand on the goat and MILOS will slay the goat.

70 – **DECLARATION OF WAR/ASSUMPTION OF POWER:** Christine conquers her fear and helps to summon the Lamia. The Lamia vows to take Christine to hell.

75 –Lamia wreaks havoc, possesses Milos and almost kills Christine but she evades him.

76 – Shaun casts the Lamia out of Milos and she dies.

78 – **END OF ACT TWO TURN:** It's not over. The Lamia is still alive – Christine must give the curse to another by giving them the button; Rham Jas puts it in a white envelope.

DECISION: Christine will find a subject to curse.

ACT THREE

80 – Christine and Clay driving; Clay's papers fall on the floor of the car over the envelope.

84 – Christine tries to give Stu the envelope but can't do it.

85 – **TRUE PT. OF NO RETURN** – Christine formulates the plan to give the cursed button back to Mrs. Ganush; she digs up Ganush's grave in the pouring rain.

88-89 – **CLIMAX (EXTERNAL):** Christine shoves the envelope in corpse's mouth. The grave fills up with water, she's knocked out, but escapes, alive.

90 – **CLIMAX (INTERNAL):** At home, safe. Mr. Jacks leaves message; he caught Stu, fired him. <u>Christine got the job</u>!

91-93 – **EPILOGUE:** She meets Clay at Union Station to go on a romantic getaway (he has an engagement ring in his pocket). She admits to Clay that she made the decision to deny Mrs. Ganush's loan. Clay pulls out her button! It got mixed up with his liberty quarter, in similar white envelopes. <u>Christine is dragged to hell</u>!

As Good As It Gets is just flat-out great screenwriting. It balances a large ensemble of speaking roles with a rock-solid active structure, shows character through action, and gives us some of the most wickedly delicious dialogue of Jack Nicholson's long career (a tall order). It's not afraid to get ugly, while being absolutely hilarious. It's long, but it never drags. I encourage you to watch it again if you haven't seen it in a while.

AS GOOD AS IT GETS (1997)

Story by Mark Andrus
Written by Mark Andrus & James L. Brooks
Directed by James L. Brooks
Running Time: 139 mins.

BASIC STORY MAP

PROTAGONIST: MELVIN UDALL: 50's, shut-in, rich novelist in NYC

Misbehavior: Obsessive-Compulsive disorder

Skill: Good at helping people (once he finally does it)

Flaw/Achilles Heel: Lack of human compassion

FALSE GOAL: To isolate himself

EXTERNAL GOAL: To belittle Simon / Be a good friend to him

INTERNAL GOAL: To use Carol / Win over Carol as a girlfriend

MAIN DRAMATIC CONFLICT: Melvin's pessimism

THEME: Don't let pessimism rule you.

CENTRAL DRAMATIC QUESTION: Can Melvin learn to love others?

ENDING: Melvin offers Simon his home and gets together with Carol.

ARC: Melvin goes from isolationist jerk to friend and lover, learning that to receive happiness and support he must first give of himself.

LOGLINE

An obsessive-compulsive, homophobic novelist must help his gay artist neighbor in order to win over the single mother he secretly loves.

FULL STORY MAP

STORY ENGINES

ACT 1: Melvin's isolated world is challenged by his gay neighbor and his sassy waitress.

ACT 2A: Melvin must take care of his neighbor's dog and get Carol back to work. He must restore order to his once pristine world but events are conspiring against him.

ACT 2B: Melvin must win Simon and Carol's trust. They bond, leaving him alone.

ACT 3: Melvin must commit to being more open, less selfish and to care for Simon and Carol if he truly wants happiness.

THE BEAT SHEET
(note: this is not a complete scene list)

ACT ONE

1 – **OPENING:** MELVIN UDALL stuffs his neighbor SIMON'S dog down the trash chute. When Simon finds out it was Melvin, he tells him "Mr. Udall, you don't love anything."

Central Dramatic Question: Can Melvin learn to love others?

9 – **INCITING INCIDENT (EXTERNAL):** Frank threatens Melvin to be nice to Simon or he will hurt him.

10 – Intro: CAROL the waitress

13 – **INCITING INCIDENT (INTERNAL):** Melvin makes a terrible remark to CAROL about her sick son.

22 – **STRONG MOVEMENT FORWARD:** Melvin asks Carol about her son, his first gesture of interest in others.

27 – **END OF ACT ONE TURN:** After Simon is attacked, Frank leaves Simon's dog Verdell with Melvin.

28 – **DECISION**: Melvin begrudgingly feeds the dog bacon to push it away, but the dog likes it. Melvin begins to care for another living creature.

ACT TWO-A

35 – **FIRST TRIAL / FIRST CASUALTY:** The dog is taken away and Melvin is devastated.

42 – Carol is not at work and Melvin gets kicked out of the restaurant by the Manager.

45 – **COMBAT:** Melvin shows up at Carol's door. She freaks out.

Melvin pays for his doctor to treat Carol's son. Carol is initially reluctant to accept the help but her mother convinces her to take it.

61 – **MIDPOINT (EXTERNAL):** Melvin tries to help Simon by showing him how to win Verdell over with bacon. This fails and the dog prefers Melvin.

66 – **MIDPOINT (INTERNAL):** Carol tells Melvin "I'm not going to sleep with you, ever."

ACT TWO-B

76 – **DECLARATION OF WAR / ASSUMPTION OF POWER:** Melvin agrees to drive Simon to Baltimore, as a way to win over Carol.

79 – Melvin uses Carol's guilt to get her to go on trip with him and Simon.

85 – **END OF ACT TWO TURN (EXTERNAL):** The three go on a road-trip.

87 – **END OF ACT TWO TURN (INTERNAL):** Simon tells the personal story of his father kicking him out.

90 – **DECISION**: Melvin tells his own sob story to try to make a connection with them; it fails. They bond, he's left out, hitting bottom.

ACT THREE

92 – Carol asks Melvin out on a date.

100 – **TRUE POINT OF NO RETURN:** Melvin: "You make me want to be a better man."
(Melvin takes a risk and reveals his interest to Carol)

102 – Carol kisses Melvin (her True Pt. of No Return).

104 – Melvin blows it by insulting her and admitting he wanted to use her; she storms out.

107 – Simon sketches Carol, calls his parents and tells them he doesn't need their money and he wants to reconcile (Simon's True Pt. of No Return).

121 – **CLIMAX (EXTERNAL):** Melvin lets Simon stay with him, and he turns to Simon for help.

123 – Simon stands up to Melvin (his Climax). Tells Melvin to "go to her."

125 – Melvin takes Simon's advice and offers him his home to stay.

130 – **CLIMAX (INTERNAL):** Melvin appreciates and praises Carol. She finally accepts him, warts and all. He grabs her (getting over his germaphobia) and kisses her!

133 – FADE OUT. [No Epilogue]

Sunset Boulevard is the classic tale of a desperate screenwriter who gets seduced by an insane silent movie star. (We've all been there, right?)

Cynical, thrilling, funny, satirical, ironic, the list of ways to describe this masterpiece can go on. It delivers one of the great screen villains, Norma Desmond, and one of the classic Film Noir protagonists, Joe Gillis. Notice how Joe thinks he's in control but the balance of power continues to shift in Norma's favor.

It's dated at times, but its achievement remains the same: dark, economical storytelling at its best.

SUNSET BOULEVARD (1950)
Written by Charles Brackett, Billy Wilder, D.M. Marshman Jr.
Directed by Billy Wilder
Running Time: 110 minutes

BASIC STORY MAP

PROTAGONIST: JOE GILLIS, struggling screenwriter

Misbehavior: Cynical

Skill: Good writer

Flaw/Achilles Heel: Materialistic

EXTERNAL GOAL: To write the script for Norma Desmond to jump-start his career

INTERNAL GOAL: To use Norma for money/ to be with Betty

MAIN DRAMATIC CONFLICT: Norma

THEME: Greed kills

CENTRAL DRAMATIC QUESTION: How does Joe end up dead in the pool?

ENDING: Joe rejects Betty and tries to leave the house but Norma shoots him.

ARC: Joe goes from a penniless, desperate screenwriter to sacrificing his dignity to sell out to Norma to a final attempt to escape, which ends in tragedy.

LOGLINE

A desperate screenwriter gets seduced into the lavish home of a former silent movie star and is made to cater to her whims at the cost of his soul.

FULL STORY MAP

STORY ENGINES

ACT 1: Joe strikes a deal with Norma Desmond out of desperation.

ACT 2A: Joe gets seduced by Norma into her lavish but delusional world.

ACT 2B: Joe slips out of the house to write with Betty and they kiss.

ACT 3: Joe tries to escape but is gunned down. Norma goes insane, finally achieving what she believes is her comeback.

THE BEAT SHEET
(note: this is not a complete scene list)

ACT ONE

0-1:30 Opening Titles Sequence: JOE GILLIS narrates as we see police cars with sirens on. A murder has been reported; an old time star is involved. He will tell us the facts of the story so you don't have to read about it in the tabloids.

2 – **OPENING**: Body in pool, shot three times. A movie writer. He always wanted a pool. He got it, but the price turned out to be high. The dead body is Joe.

3 – Joe is a struggling writer in his tiny studio apartment in Hollywood. Repo men come to take his car, giving him until noon tomorrow to get the money or he's in trouble.

6 – **INCITING INCIDENT (INTERNAL)**: In a producer's office at Paramount, script reader BETTY SHAEFER walks in, trashing Joe's script, not knowing he's in the room.

10 – Joe's AGENT dumps him.

11 – **INCITING INCIDENT (EXTERNAL):** Joe is chased by the Repo Men in his car. He pulls into a strange driveway off of Sunset to evade them.

12 – Joe is ready to give up and move back to Dayton, Ohio, when he's summoned by the voice of a WOMAN, mistaking him for someone else. The stoic butler, MAX, lets him in.

15 – Joe meets NORMA DESMOND, former silent movie star. She wants him to bury her dead chimp in a white coffin with a satin lining.

16 – Joe: "You're Norma Desmond. You were in silent movies, you used to be big." Norma: "I am big. It's the *pictures* that got small."

20 – **STRONG MOVEMENT FORWARD:** Joe begins to read Norma's handwritten manuscript for *Salome*, her big return to the silver screen, as MAX serves champagne and caviar and Norma watches him. It's awful, but Joe comes up with a plan.

22 – Norma hires Joe to write it but he must stay the night to finish reading.

27 – **END OF ACT ONE TURN:** Joe wakes up in the morning to find all of his belongings in the room, as if he were moving in.

28 – Norma has paid Joe's back rent. He's pissed but she's got him over a barrel; he needs the job.

29 – **DECISION:** He takes the job and starts writing in the mansion as Norma hovers.

30 – Norma makes him re-insert a scene he threw out so she's in every scene.

ACT TWO-A

32 – Time passes – they watch her movies on her private movie screen, play cards with Buster Keaton and other silent movie stars. It's like time stopped in her mansion.

35-37 – Norma lavishes gifts upon Joe, like a tuxedo with tails for her upcoming New Year's Eve party. He's becoming her pet.

38 – **FIRST TRIAL:** Joe is moved into the main house, into the room of Norma's former husbands.

39-40 – **FIRST CASUALTY:** Max points out there are no locks on the doors in the house because Norma has attempted suicide in the past. He reveals that he sends her fan letters, maintaining her fantasy that she is still a huge star.

43 – New Year's Eve party in the mansion; no other guests are coming; it's just them!

45 – **COMBAT**: Joe blows up, can't take it anymore; he has a life of his own! She slaps him, runs to her room. He leaves.

47 – New Year's party at Artie Green's apartment. Betty Shaefer is Artie's girlfriend.

50 – Betty likes one of Joe's stories, wants to collaborate with him on a script. They flirt, make a connection.

52 – Joe calls Max; Norma cut her wrists! Joe rushes back to the mansion.

55 – **MIDPOINT (EXTERNAL):** Norma threatens to attempt suicide again. Joe is overcome with guilt. As midnight comes and *Auld Lang Syne* plays, Joe goes to Norma and kisses her. They are now lovers.

59-60 **MIDPOINT (INTERNAL)** – Joe runs into Artie and Betty at Schwab's Pharmacy. Betty has got interest from Sheldrake in the script; he refuses to collaborate.

ACT TWO-B

64 – After Norma gets a call from Paramount, they drive onto the lot to see Cecil B. DeMille.

69 – Norma gets mobbed by crew members on the set, feeding her ego and delusion.

70 – DeMille finds out that Paramount is only interested in renting her car. He doesn't have the heart to tell her.

74 – **DECLARATION OF WAR:** Joe comes up with a script idea for Betty that she loves, but he still refuses to write it with her. She and Artie are engaged but he's out of town on a shoot.

76 – Norma goes through a grueling beauty regimen to get ready for her big-screen comeback that she's convinced will be directed by DeMille.

79 –**ASSUMPTION OF POWER:** Joe slips out to write with Betty at her office at night.

80-82 – Betty finds his cigarette case signed by Norma. He lies. They almost kiss.

85 – Max warns Joe not to hurt Norma. Max reveals that he was a former director who discovered her when she was 16, and also her first husband!

87 – **END OF ACT TWO TURN (EXTERNAL):** Norma finds Joe's script and seethes with jealousy when she sees Betty Schaefer's name on the title page!

89 – **END OF ACT TWO TURN (INTERNAL):** Betty tells Joe that Artie wants her to get married right away. She's no longer in love with Artie because she's in love with Joe.

DECISION: They kiss.

ACT THREE

91 – Same night, Norma calls Betty to warn her about Joe.

92 – Joe grabs phone, tells Betty to come visit him at the house to discover his secret.

94 – **TRUE POINT OF NO RETURN (Internal):** Betty arrives at the mansion. Joe gives her the tour of the mansion, confessing his sordid situation.

98 – Betty asks him to leave with her; he refuses and she leaves, in tears.

99 – Joe packs to leave; he's going to start over back in Dayton, Ohio.

100 – **TRUE POINT OF NO RETURN (External)**: Norma shows him her gun, threatening suicide again.

101 – Joe tells her the truth about Paramount and Max's phony fan letters.

102 – He tries to get her to wake up but she's lost her mind, babbling that she's the greatest star in the world. She finally cracks, for good.

103 – **CLIMAX**: Norma shoots Joe three times. He falls in the pool.

104 – **EPILOGUE**: Back to Joe's narration, his body in the pool BOOKENDING from the opening image – the cops arrive at the house.

107 – Norma, catatonic, walks out to see the press cameras. Max directs Norma in a scene from *Salome* to get her to come downstairs.

109 – Norma, completely insane, moves toward the camera for her "Close-up."

110 – End

Acknowledgments

Thank you to all of my students and clients for your hard work, inspiration, courage and trust in me.

Special thanks to my crack researchers, a.k.a. "Story Mappers:" James Robert Martin, Dustin Tanner, Mary Szmagaj, Guy McDouall, Mike Murphy and expert editorial assistants, Ron Calvisi and Brendan McCall.

Thank you to all of the talented and supportive writers who have been in and out of The Writers' Building over the years.

Thank you to all of the professionals in the entertainment industry that I have worked for, with and learned so much from and to all of the professionals mentioned in the "From The Trenches" sections.

Big love to all of the cats that have walked across my keyboard over the years as I compiled this material. You know who you are!

For my Mother for her undying support of my creative side and for my Father for his financial contributions to my at-times creatively starved bank account.

Finally, this book is dedicated to my Copy Editor's continued pursuit of her literary dreams. May you write happily, write well and be fulfilled in your creative endeavors, Ms. Nicole Schlosser.

"...combines expert analysis with incredible credentials and experience..."

-Script Magazine

MAKE YOUR SCRIPT GREAT!

Dear Screenwriters, young and old, new and experienced, local and abroad:

We will always need great stories and great writers to write them.

It doesn't matter if you make money at it—if you ENJOY IT, then DO IT.

I hope you can be a part of this amazing tradition of storytelling in its most powerful form: movies, television and digital media.

As a purchaser of this book, I am happy to extend to you **discounts** and **special offers** on my consultation services, coaching, classes and other publications. On my website, you will find more collections of Story Maps ("Booster Packs"), free downloads and more information about how I can help you to get your screenplay in "submission ready" shape.

Good Luck and Happy Writing!

Daniel P. Calvisi

Website www.ActFourScreenplays.com

Blog www.actfourscreenplays.com/blog

YouTube www.youtube.com/actfourscreenplays

Facebook www.facebook.com/storymaps

Twitter www.twitter.com/storymapsdan

CPSIA information can be obtained
at www.ICGtesting.com
Printed in the USA
LVHW040329250519
619123LV00001B/61/P

9 780983 626602